BENJAMIN BRITTEN

Britten
photographed at Aldeburgh in 1974 by Victor Parker (New York)

PICTURES FROM A LIFE

Benjamin Britten

1913-1976

A PICTORIAL BIOGRAPHY

COMPILED BY

Donald Mitchell

WITH THE ASSISTANCE OF

John Evans

Charles Scribner's Sons

·

New York

CONTENTS

Library of Congress Catalog Card Number 78 – 59150.

ISBN 0-684-15974-0

1 3 5 7 9 11 13 15 17 19   I/C   20 18 16 14 12 10 8 6 4 2

To

Barbara, Robert and Beth

in memory of their brother

Ben

Britten, at least during the years I knew him, showed a distinct dislike for the camera, especially when it was pointing at *him*.* Yet he was a much photographed man, and the more celebrated he became, so did the rolls of film accumulate, the files of negatives and prints grow thicker. I cannot begin to estimate accurately how many photographs and photographic sources my assistant John Evans and I have looked through, but they must run into many hundreds. I cannot claim to have consulted every source, and indeed it was never my intention or ambition to scrutinize all the known photographic sources, let alone to seek out all the unknown ones. To achieve such comprehensiveness would have required many years of further research and resulted in a book of unmanageable dimensions. Moreover, there comes a point in the gathering together of photographs - the recognition of it depends more on intuition than on precise mathematics – when the adding of yet more photographs does not automatically bring with it a proportional increase in information or enlightenment. On the contrary, an overwhelming mass of material can lead to a blurring of the clear image one hopes to project, to masking rather than articulating the continuity of the narrative. I think in fact that our sub-title, 'Pictures from a Life', is perfectly self-explicit with its implication that it is not necessarily the whole life that we attempt to present. I am happy to live with our necessary gaps and omissions, but have tried to cover these in another way by providing the extensive Chronological Table at the back of the book which offers as it were a continuous *curriculum vitae*.

There is no point it seems to me in dwelling on the gaps, which readers (and reviewers, doubtless) will alight on for themselves without my assistance. But perhaps there is one omission that I ought to mention. We unfold here pictures from a *life*, and though Britten's works naturally form a permanent and major topic throughout, there is no attempt on our part to document them all, not even all the operas. Where there was a good or revealing or characteristic or entertaining or little-known or particularly informative photograph – and those roughly were the principles that guided our selection – then we chose to include it, no matter whether a work, or which work, was involved. (There were exceptions, of course, like the *War Requiem*, which demanded installation as a matter of documentary right.) Moreover, we felt, if the operas are to be adequately recorded they really require a pictorial book of their own, especially if it is to take account, as it should, of John Piper's original stage designs. We hear, as we go to press, that Mr David Herbert is in the process of putting just such a book together,† and are glad that our own independently reached decision means that there will be no needless duplication of effort or contents.

To use, as I have above, the word 'research' in connection with a picture book may strike some as unduly solemn or even pretentious. What is to be 'discovered' other than the picture itself? Would that the task of the pictorial biographer were as simple as the asking of that question implies. It may be that every picture tells a story, as the old saying has it. We have found, however, that the story will often change with the viewer. This,

---

*He would have been amused, I think, to appear in this book in two guises: as frequent subject of the camera, and also, in his youth at least, as a keen photographer. The carefully captioned albums he kept in those days have been among our most valuable sources.

†To be published by Messrs Hamish Hamilton.

no doubt, is to be expected, memory being as fallible as it is; and photographs – though they seem so real, so immediate, so precisely placed at the moment the shutter clicks – prove after the passage of time to be subject to exactly the same vagaries, uncertainties and confusions of interpretation as every other form of human documentation. There is nothing surprising perhaps about the speed with which even the very recent past covers or obscures its tracks: dates dissolve, locations blur, events and identities become unstable, indistinguishable or ambiguous, faces disappear. *X* thinks that is how he *may* have looked thirty-five years ago, but is wonderfully confident that it is *Y* who stands on his right. When we show the photograph to *Y*, he not only dismisses the suggestion that it is he who stands on *X*'s right but is also wholly convinced that *X* has mis-identified himself, and enlists the aid of *X*'s own family to support him in his view. As a consequence, *X* retires, while *Y* has excluded himself. We are left with our voids and blanks, indicated by 'not identified'. If I spell out an example of the extreme difficulties we have occasionally encountered, it is not just to amuse (or to excuse in advance our inevitable errors) but rather to remind those who consult this book that, Eric Walter White's painstaking study of Britten apart, of which we have made continuous use, this is the first attempt to document the composer's life – better, perhaps, his private and working lives – in detail. There is no doubt that a great deal of new information is offered here, based on original source material. But we shall certainly have made mistakes and guessed wrong from time to time or drawn the wrong conclusions; and we shall be glad to hear from those who can put us or our captions right.

However, though we may have researched diligently, comprehensiveness was still not our aim. If not comprehensiveness, then what? First, as I have already hinted, we have been guided by the interest of a photograph *qua* photograph, and have not been wholly swayed by the interest or importance of the subject. It is curious, in fact, how often an interesting event or occasion or exotic context will emerge as a very dull photograph, and this we have tried to avoid. Second, we have, despite all the admitted omissions, tried to give an impression of the scope of a creative life of quite exceptional richness and diversity, and – not less – of a unique order of fertility and unremitting hard work. We ourselves, I think, came to be progressively more and more astonished by the pictorial evidence of this prodigal inventiveness and energy that our researches revealed. We hope, if nothing else, to have succeeded in marking out the span of Britten's life, from its very first days to its very last, and to have indicated *en route* the intensity with which the life was lived. (It is not, I think, fanciful to recognize that it is this quality of intensity that so often proves to be the common factor that unites a wealth of portraits otherwise very different and contrasted in expression. That the intensity was *there* from the very beginning can surely not be doubted, now that the marvellous photographs from Britten's childhood are available to us.)

Third, and lastly, we have tried to bring forward important periods in Britten's life that, relatively speaking, are unfamiliar, particularly in pictorial terms. The very early years in Lowestoft are an obvious case, as are the years he spent in London first as a student and later as a young and incredibly industrious and versatile composer, making what have proved to be historic contributions to the theatre, to film and to radio, and making, too, remarkable friendships that were to have a profound influence on his future composing. We have scarcely done more than touch the margins of the vast mass of material that belongs to the topic of Britten and the 1930s; none the less, I think we show clearly and for the first time in some substance just how significant was the role played by Britten in the decade distinguished by the activities of W. H. Auden, Alberto Cavalcanti, William Coldstream, Rupert Doone, John Grierson, Christopher Isherwood, Louis MacNeice, Robert Medley, John Piper, Paul Rotha, Basil Wright, and many, many others. In the ultimate roll-call of the 1930s Britten must have as prominent a place as any of his illustrious contemporaries.

Then too there are the American years, from 1939 to 1942, which have never before, we think, been documented in comparable detail. These are years significant enough in musical achievement to warrant independent attention. The collaboration with Auden on *Paul Bunyan* reminds us usefully, as do all the film, radio and theatre scores from the immediately preceding London period, that *Peter Grimes* did not spring out of the earth without a great deal of arduous preparation of the soil. Likewise the two remarkable years at Glyndebourne which saw the composition and first productions of *Lucretia* and *Herring*. Along with and out of that experience were to develop many of the concerns that were to preoccupy Britten in the decades to come and which, with the help of his closest friends and collaborators, he was to fulfil in and around Aldeburgh, in the county where he was born and where he was to die, the two events which inevitably frame this book. But rather like the 'frame' in one of Britten's own operas – e.g. in *Lucretia* or *Budd* – while not underestimating its importance, it is what happens in between that counts.

Donald Mitchell

Lagonissi, Greece
April 1978

ACKNOWLEDGEMENTS

Without the generous help of the following friends, who allowed me use of their archives, their memories and their time, this book would not have been possible: Sir Peter Pears; Miss Barbara Britten; Mr Robert Britten; Mrs Beth Welford; Miss Rosamund Strode; Mrs Beata Sauerlander (Beata Mayer, New York); Princess Margaret of Hesse and the Rhine; my co-Executors of the Britten Estate.

I also wish to record my particular thanks to the following individuals: Mr Richard Alston; Mrs John Bodley; Mr and Mrs Antonio Brosa; Mrs Queenie Burgess; Miss Sally Cavender; Mr Aaron Copland; Miss Joan Cross CBE; Mr Brian Dickie; Mr Anthony Fell; Mr Howard Ferguson; Mrs Sylvia Goldstein (New York); Dr Sergei Hackel; Mrs Arthur Harrison; Dr Jonathan Harvey; Mr Derek Hill; Miss Imogen Holst; Mr Christopher Isherwood; Mr Hans Keller; Mr Tony Kitzinger; Mr Philip Larkin; Mr Remo Lauricella; Mrs Walter Lippincott; Mr Nigel Luckhurst; Mr Robert Medley; Mr Edward Mendelson (Yale); Mrs Kathleen Mitchell; Mrs John Mundy; Miss Daphne Oliver; Miss Helen O'Neil; Miss Judith Osborne; Mr and Mrs Jack Phipps; Mr John Piper; Mr Stuart Pope (New York); Mrs Mary Potter; Mr Bernard Richards; Mr Mstislav Rostropovitch; Mr and Mrs. Peter du Sautoy; Mr William Servaes; Mr J. D. Sewell; Miss Bette Snapp (New York); Miss Rita Thomson; Mrs Jeremy Thorpe; Mr and Mrs Theodor Uppman (New York); Sir Paul Wright; Miss Sophie Wyss.

I am also indebted to the following organizations: The Aldeburgh Festival; Boosey and Hawkes, London; Boosey and Hawkes, Inc., New York; the BBC; the Britten-Pears Library, Aldeburgh; the Central Music Library, Westminster; the Decca Record Company Ltd.; the English Music Theatre (formerly the English Opera Group); the English National Opera Company (formerly Sadler's Wells Opera); Faber and Faber Ltd.; Faber Music Ltd.; Glyndebourne Opera; *The Guardian*; the National Portrait Gallery, London; the New York Public Library (Berg Collection); the Royal College of Music; the Royal Opera House, Covent Garden; Sotheby's.

The sources of the photographs are gratefully acknowledged at the end of the book. We have made every effort to trace copyright owners and shall be glad to hear from those that we have been unable to locate or have inadvertently omitted.   D.M.

1 An early photograph of Britten's father, Robert Victor, probably before his marriage at the age of twenty-three. *Photo* Wm. Plumb, Maidenhead.

2 An early portrait study of Britten's mother, Edith Rhoda Hockey, before her marriage. She was probably in her early twenties and living in London. She married at the age of twenty-seven. *Photo* Alexander Bassano, London.

3 *Lowestoft*. Edward Benjamin Britten aged four years and two months. (*See also caption to No.24.*)

4 *Maidenhead.* Family group. In the back row, Britten's father and Aunt Flo (one of Mr Britten's sisters, like Aunts Jessie and Louise below). Mrs Britten sits next to Grandma Britten, *née* Charlotte Ginders. At the front sit, left to right, Barbara Britten, the composer's elder sister, Aunt Jessie, Robert Britten, his elder brother, and Aunt Louise.

5 Aunt Julia Ginders, Britten's great-aunt. Great-aunt Julia was the sister of Britten's grandmother, Charlotte Ginders.

6 Aunt Queenie. She was Sarah Fanny Hockey, Mrs Britten's youngest sister. (*See No. 27.*)

7 *Lowestoft.* A portrait of Mrs Britten after her marriage. *Photo* Boughton, Lowestoft.

8 A pen-and-ink drawing of the family house at Lowestoft – 21 Kirkley Cliff Road – preserved among Britten's papers. (*See also No.11.*)

9 *Lowestoft.* Britten's father and Aunt Jessie on safety bicycles. The passenger was Robert.

10 'Pop' in the garden at Lowestoft.

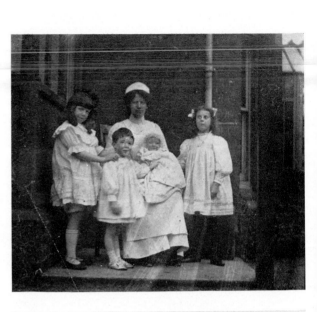

11 21 Kirkley Cliff Road, Lowestoft, where Britten was born on 22 November 1913. It was here that Britten's father had his dental practice.

12 *Lowestoft, c.1909.* Left to right, Barbara, Robert, Nanny (the baby is Elizabeth (Beth), the younger of Britten's two sisters), and a cousin, Elsie Hockey.

13 *Lowestoft, 1914.* Britten, aged one, with his nanny, Mrs Scarce, *née* Walker.

14 *Lowestoft, c.1915.* Britten aged about two.

15 Britten aged about three, taking part in a dramatic performance of *The Water Babies* at the Sparrow's Nest Theatre, Lowestoft. He sits on the lap of his mother, who was playing the role of Mrs Do-as-you-would-be-done-by. Britten recalled in later life that he was 'dressed in skin-coloured tights, with madly curly hair, trying desperately to remember the lines spoken by Tom the water-baby'. (From the speech he made on receiving the Freedom of Lowestoft on 28 July 1951. *See No.247.*)

16 *Lowestoft*. Robert with a friend.

17 Barbara aged about fourteen or fifteen. *Photo* Edgar & Co., Lowestoft.

18 *Lowestoft*. Britten on Aunt Effie's lap, aged five or six? At her side, Robert. Aunt Effie was one of Mrs Britten's three younger sisters (the others were Queenie, the youngest, and Daisy). Daisy died of tuberculosis shortly after her marriage.

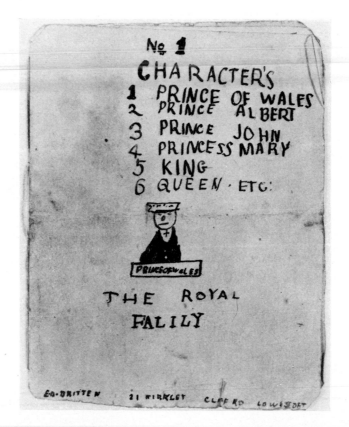

No 1

CHARACTER'S
1 PRINCE OF WALES
2 PRINCE ALBERT
3 PRINCE JOHN
4 PRINCESS MARY
5 KING
6 QUEEN· ETC:

THE ROYAL
FALILY

EⱯ·BRITTEN   21 KIRKLEY   CLIFF RD LOWESTOFT

I   SCEN 1 A BDROOD·IN THE
PALACE PRINCE JOHN IN BED AND
THE QUEEN BY THE SIDE OF HIM

G) I HOPE YOU ARE BETTER
PJ) I DONT NO MUMMY
        ENTER PRINCE OF WALES
PW   WHY WHAT ARE YOU MY LITTLE
MAN
PJ) IM ILL
Q   YES HE IS
PW OH IS HE WHAT IS THE MATTER WITH
    HIM
Q) I DONT NO

PW OH WHO IS IT HALLO

ALBERT WHERE IS MARY
P) ASHES COMEING

SCEN 2   2

SAME BEDROOD JOHN DEAD

Q CRYING OH
JOHNS DEAD POOR ME
K) OH HOW
Q HE WAS ILL
K) OH
Q) YES
K) WHY WAS HO ILL
Q) COURSE he HAD ~ FITS
K) OH OH OH
Q WHY WHY
K) MY TOE TOE AND ROE ROE

MY TOE TOE AND ROE ROE
K) IMM NOT (Q) YOU ARE·
K) IMM NOT (Q) YOU ARE NOT (K) AH AH
WE WE (Q) OH

SCEN 3
BALL ROOM AT BARBADOES

P)W WHY MISS BRITTEN
M)B YES PRINCE I AM
MISS BRITTEN
P)W GOODBYE MISS BRITTEN
        EXIT MISS BRITTEN

    SCEN 4
ON THE WAY FROM
    BARBADOES
(T) WELL PRINCE ARE YOU
READY TO - BE DUCKED
P)W WHAT ME BE DUCKED
(T) YES ME DEAR PRINCE
AND YOUR BROTHER TOO
P)W OH NOT MY BROTHER

SCEN 5
ON THE WAY TO BARBADOES
CT NOW TO BE DUCKED. YOU, TO. ALBERT
P)W NO
P)A NOT ME OR YOU
P)W NO YOUARE NOT GOING
TOO DUCKED ALBERT
CT YES I AM
P)W NOW YOU ARN'T
    SCENE ROYAL TRAIN
    P)W OH YES IM GOING BY THIS
TRAIN AND ALBERT TOO
SM PORTOR PORTOR HERE COMES THE
ROYAL PARTY BE READY TO STAND
A TENTION
P) PUFF, PUFF, PUFF) HOW THE
TRUM PETS BLOW

5 MAKE — UP
P)W SHOULD HAVE A BLUE SAILOR
SUIT AND LONG TROUSERS IN,
SCEN 1 2 3 4 AND 5 AND 6 he
SHOULD HAVE A TWEED SUIT AND
P)A SHOULD HAVE A BLUE ONE TO
PS)M)S SHOULD HAVE A
CARDBOARD CROWN
KING IN A RED DRESS
QUEEN IN A BLUE DRESS
AND A CARD BOARD CROWN

    THE END

19 *Lowestoft, c.1920-21.* A play written – and 'published' – by Britten, probably at the age of six or seven. The topic, 'The Royal Falily [*sic*]', was a favourite one. We reproduce the title page and the complete text, in Scene 2 of which appears what must have been the composer's first attempt at incidental music. The last page makes clear that the young dramatist had a proper care for the details of costume design.

20 *Lowestoft*, Britten on his scooter. He looks younger, however, than the date in his brother's photograph album ('1920/1') suggests.
21 *Lowestoft*. On the beach. Britten aged about seven.
22 Britten, aged six, in the garden at Lowestoft. (*Compare, however, No. 26.*)
23 *Lowestoft, c. 1922*. On the beach. Britten was aged about eight. With him were his father's secretary, Miss Haes, and his sister, Beth. Britten's companion was a family friend, Elizabeth Boyd.

24 *Lowestoft*. Britten, aged nine years and ten months, dressed for prep school. A photograph originally in the possession of Britten's nanny, hence the detailed information about his age.
25 *Lowestoft, c.1923*. Britten, aged about nine, reading in the garden. *Photo Barbara Britten*.
26 The young tennis player. Britten, aged about eight, with Aunt Jessie.

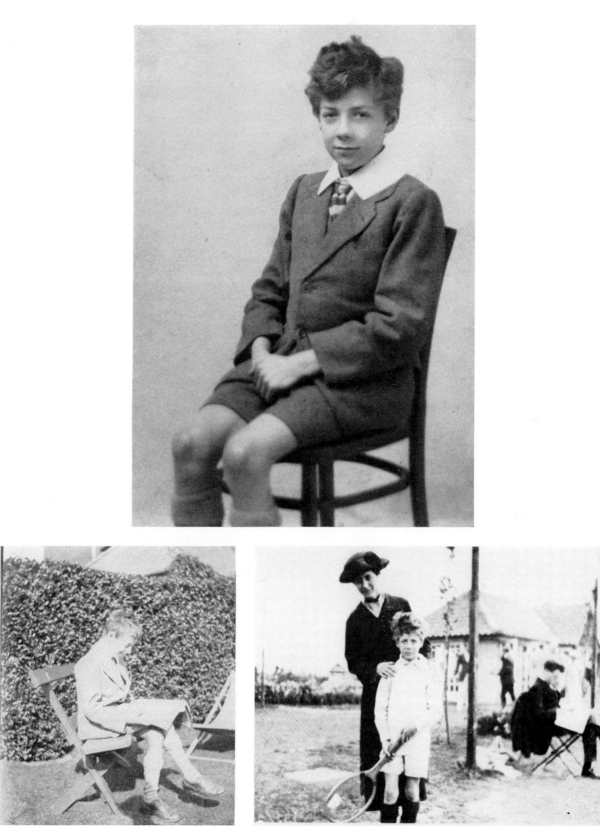

27 A portrait miniature of Britten aged about nine, painted by Aunt Queenie (*see No.6*). This was given by Britten to the poet William Plomer (1903-1973; *see No. 257*), the librettist of *Gloriana* and the three Church Parables, who bequeathed it to the National Portrait Gallery, London. *Photo* National Portrait Gallery.

28 The title page of two songs composed – and again 'published' (*see No.19*) – by E.B. Britten. The songs belong to early childhood, probably 1922-3. Britten retained an affection all his life for his setting of Longfellow's 'Beware!'.

29 The first page of what was probably the first version of 'Beware!'. (In Imogen Holst's *Britten* (1966), a fair copy of the song is reproduced on p.17.)

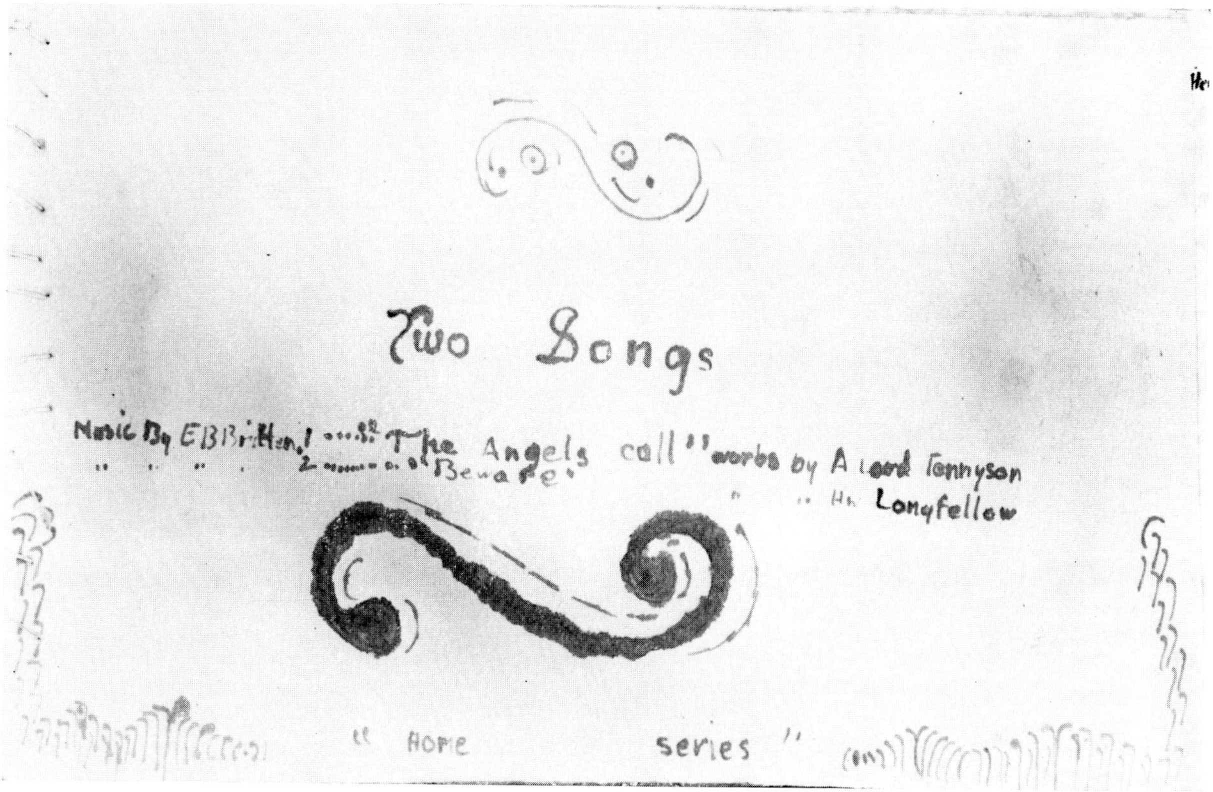

Two Songs

Music By E B Britten! ...1º The Angels call" words by A Lord Tennyson
" " " 2 ..... º Beware " " .. H. Longfellow

"Home series"

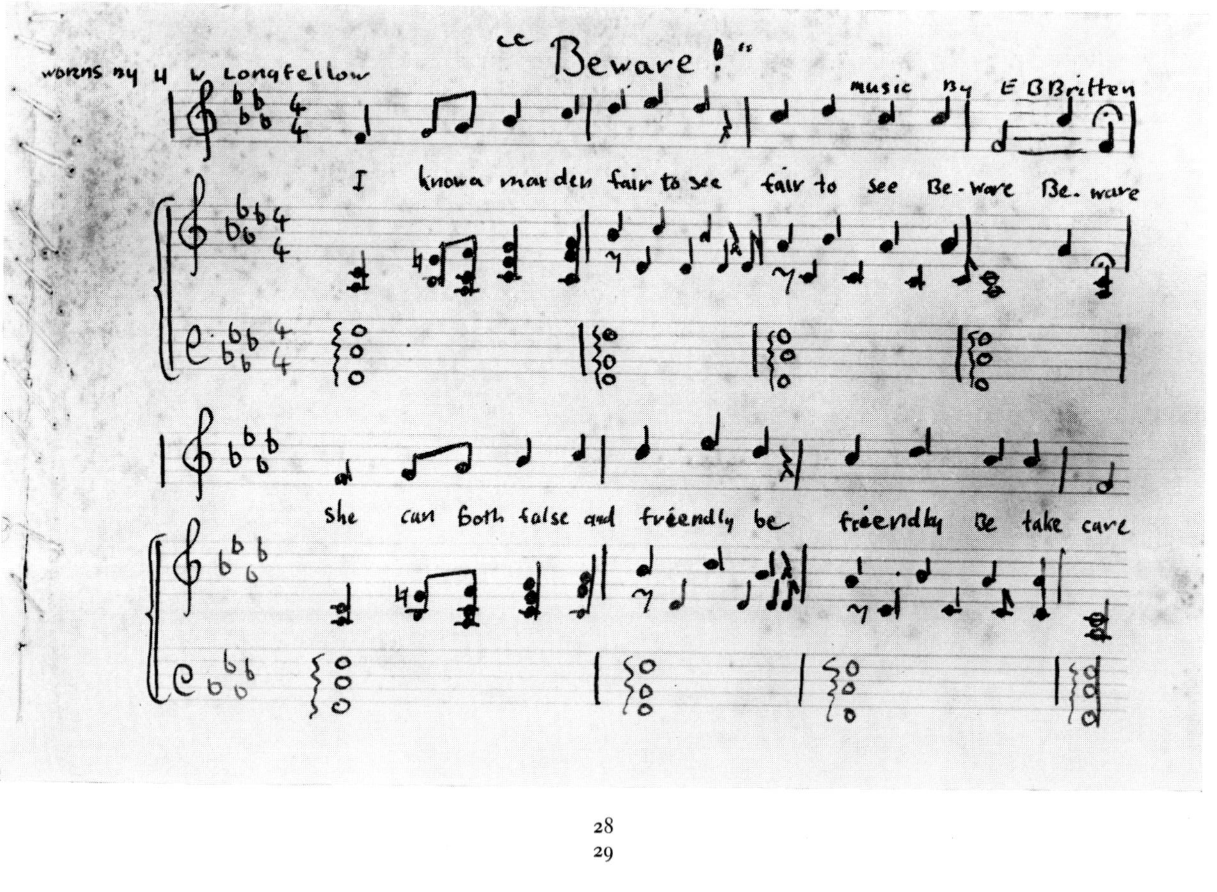

words by H W Longfellow

"Beware!"

music By E B Britten

I know a maiden fair to see fair to see Be-ware Be-ware

she can both false and friendly be friendly Be take care

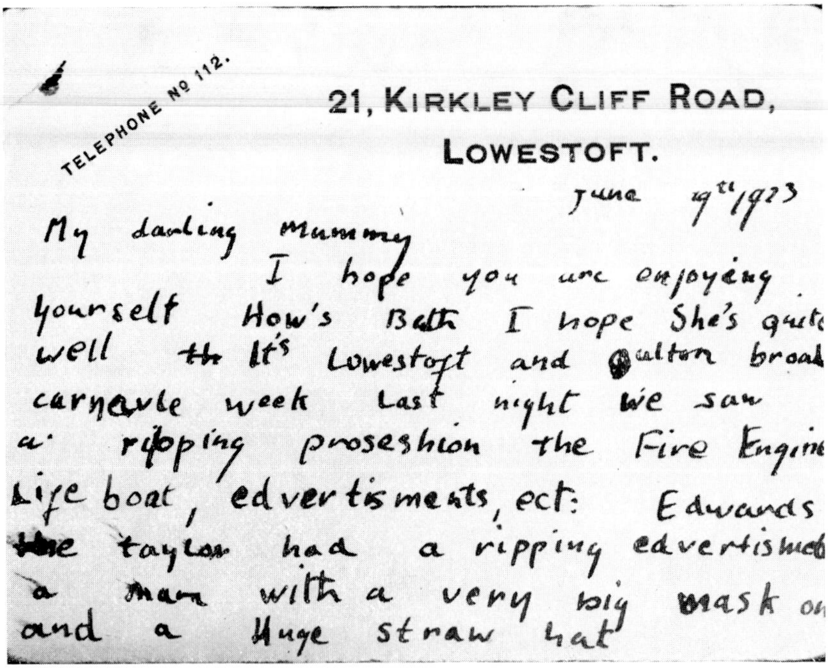

21, KIRKLEY CLIFF ROAD,
LOWESTOFT.

June 19ᵗʰ 1923

My darling mummy
I hope you are enjoying
yourself How's Beth I hope She's quite
well It's Lowestoft and Oulton broad
carneavle week Last night we saw
a ripping proseshion the Fire Engine
Life boat, edvertisments, ect: Edwards
the taylor had a ripping edvertisment
a man with a very big mask on
and a Huge straw hat

Love Bennie

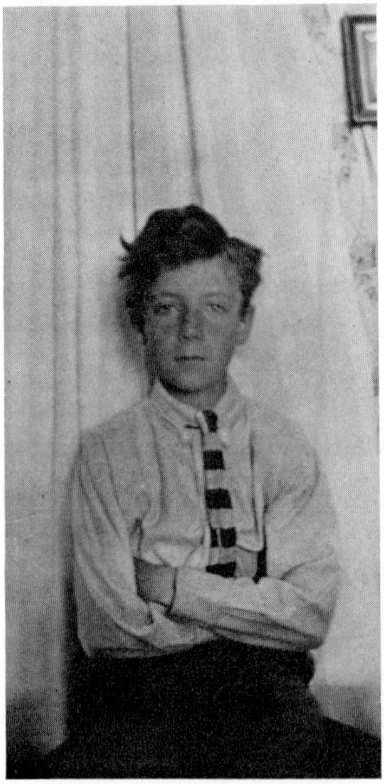

30 A letter to Mrs Britten, dated 19 June 1923. Britten was nine
years old. The drawing depicts a local carnival procession: 'Edwards:
the taylor had a ripping edvertisment a man with a very big mask on
and a Huge straw hat.'
31 Lowestoft, c.1925. Britten bowling on the playing fields of his
preparatory school, South Lodge, where he was a pupil from 1923 to
1928.
32 Lowestoft, c.1924. Britten at home, aged about eleven. Photo
Barbara Britten.

33 *South Lodge School*. A photograph of a brick on which Britten carved his initials. It was a practice common among the boys at South Lodge during the middle 1920s. *Photo* Allan Sewell.

34 South Lodge School, Lowestoft, since destroyed by fire.

35 The South Lodge cricket team with Britten, aged about eleven or twelve, standing in the back row, second from left. In the front row, fourth from left, is John Nicholson, who was to remain a lifelong friend of Britten.

36 *South Lodge School in 1923*. Sitting in the front row, fourth from left, is the nine-year-old Britten, with John Nicholson on his left.

37 *Lowestoft*. Family and friends on beach. Left to right: Rosemary
Pollard, Barbara Cameron, Mabel Austin, Britten in South Lodge
blazer, aged ten or eleven, Mrs Britten, Robert, Guitau Knowles,
Beth, Kathleen Mead and Muriel Cameron.
38 *Lowestoft, c.1927-8*. Britten with his brother Robert.
39 *Frinton-on-Sea, Essex, c.1927-8*. Britten with the family of his
school friend, Francis Barton, who is on Britten's left.

40 Britten at about fifteen years (*c*.1928-9). *Photo* Boughton,
Lowestoft.
41 Farfield House at Gresham's School, Holt, where Britten was
educated from 1928 to 1930.

42 *Arosa, Switzerland.* Britten's parents on holiday.

43 *Lowestoft.* A family group in the garden. Left to right: Barbara, Britten's father and mother, Robert (standing), Yvonne Clar, the Swiss au pair, and Britten aged about fourteen.

44 *Lowestoft, c.1929-30.* Britten, aged fifteen to sixteen, on the sea wall.

45 *London.* A photograph of Britten, *c.*1930, inscribed 'To Miss Ethel / Everlastingly gratefully / Benjamin Britten'. Miss Ethel was Ethel Astle, the local teacher with whom Britten had piano lessons

from the age of eight. It was Miss Astle's pre-preparatory school – 'Southolme' – that Britten and his sister Beth attended before he entered South Lodge. *Photo* Swaine, London.

46 *April 1928.* Three successive entries from Britten's schoolboy diary for 26, 27 and 28 April, which record a sequence of lessons with Frank Bridge in London. (Britten was still at South Lodge School.) (*See No.50.*) Britten pasted onto the page the programme of the 'wonderful Beethoven concert' on 28 April which we also reproduce.

ROYAL CHORAL SOCIETY.
Royal Albert Hall.
SATURDAY APRIL 28th AT 2.30 p.m.
BEETHOVEN CONCERT.
Egmont Overture.
MASS IN D
Pianoforte concerto in B♭ (no. 2)
Choral Fantasia

Miss DOROTHY SILK
Miss MURIEL BRUNSKILL
Mr PARRY JONES.
Mr ARTHUR CRANMER.
Piano
Mr Howard JONES
New Symphony Orchestra.
Conductor:—
DR. MALCOLM SARGENT.

OUR SMALLEST PLANTS.

The smallest plants in the whole world are probably the microbes which cause so many of our diseases. Not all microbes, of course, are plants, but the great majority of them are. Even the "worm" which causes the skin complaint called ringworm is really a microscopic plant, and not a worm at all. The little rod-like plants shown in the picture give rise to the disease called anthrax in animals and men. Each one measures only about one six-thousandth part of a millimetre in length.

47 *Friston, Sussex*. At the Bridges' home, 11-13 September 1933. To the left of Mrs Bridge stands Harold Samuel (1879-1937) who taught Britten the piano, while he was at Gresham's, in London during the holidays. (His later piano teacher, at the Royal College of Music, was Arthur Benjamin. *See No. 62*.) To the right of Frank Bridge is Howard Ferguson (*b.* 1908). The dog, to whom the group attends, was Swaffie.

48 The Bridges' house at Friston, with the water-tower close by. Britten's caption: 'May 1934 Friston Field and Tower'. *Photo* BB.

49 *Friston*. Mr and Mrs Frank Bridge and car.

50 A sketch by Marjorie Fass of the fourteen-year-old Britten completing a composition exercise for Frank Bridge at Friston. Signed 'MF 1928'.

51 *Friston*. A drawing of Frank Bridge by Marjorie Fass. Britten began private composition lessons with Bridge, in London and at Friston, in 1927 when he was thirteen.

52 *Friston*. A round composed by Britten in honour of Bridge's birthday on 26 February 1933. He wrote in his diary for that date: 'Supper at Miss Fass's, where we sing the birthday round, written by Miss Fass & music (so-called) by me (in afternoon).' In the right-hand margin of the MS, the names of those taking part in the celebration were recorded: Toni (Brosa – the violinist); Peggy (Mrs Brosa); Bill (Mrs Bridge's pet name); Bernard (Richards – the cellist); Benjie (Britten) and Marj (Fass), the last two declaring themselves to be the makers of the round. 'Franco' was Bridge. Perhaps the choice of festive key was not altogether accidental, e.g. the Bridge *Idyll* for string quartet from which Britten took the theme of his Bridge Variations (Op.10) was in E major.

53 *Friston, 1930s*. A group photograph. Front row, left to right: Frank Bridge, Peggy Brosa (*see No.84*), not identified, and Mrs Bridge. Back row, left to right: Antonio Brosa, Marjorie Fass (*see Nos. 50, 51, 54 and 135*), Christopher Alston, Britten and not identified. Christopher was the son of Audrey Alston (*see No. 74*).

54 *Friston*. A sketch of Antonio Brosa (*b. 1894*) by Marjorie Fass. (*See also No. 135.*)

55 *Sussex, 11–13 September 1933.* A shrimping party with the Bridges on the beach near Friston. Left to right: Mrs Bridge, Bridge, Ferguson and Samuel. (*Compare No. 47.*)

56 *Lowestoft, South Lodge School, 5 April 1933.* Britten's diary reads: 'I go & play cricket with South Lodge boys, up on their field. Great fun; have a glorious knock, making 33 & eventually retiring with bust bat! Not stylish cricket tho'.'

57 *London.* Mr and Mrs Frank Bridge at home, 4 Bedford Gardens, w.8. On the bookcase what was probably a portrait of Winthrop Rogers, the publisher.

58 John Ireland (1879-1962), Britten's composition teacher at the Royal College of Music where Britten was a student from 1930 to 1933. A photograph from the 1930s.

59 *London, c.1930.* An exercise by Britten, Grade V, written for 'Mr. Ireland'.

60 The Royal College of Music, Prince Consort Road, Kensington, s.w.7, *c.*1930.

61 *London, c.1933.* Britten thought this portrait was taken while he was at the College. *Photo* Hughes Studios, London.

62 Arthur Benjamin (1893-1960), the Australian-born composer, conductor and pianist, who was Britten's piano teacher at the College. The *Holiday Diary*, Op.5, for piano (1934) was dedicated by Britten to his teacher. *Photo* Frank Otley, London.

63 *London.* The programme for the Ballet Club Theatre concert on Tuesday 31 January 1933, when Britten's *Sinfonietta*, Op.1, for ten instruments received its first performance.

<table>
<tr><td>

Programme

*Concerto for Oboe and Chamber Orchestra
   in C major (1932)   *H. K. Andrews*

Allegro con moto   Slow and sustained   Allegro molto

Solo Oboe : SYLVIA SPENCER

*Sinfonietta for ten instruments (1932)
                        Benjamin Britten

Poco presto e agitato—Andante lento—Tarantella (Presto vivace)

INTERVAL

*Serenade for five wind instruments (1932)
                        Gordon Jacob

Overture—Air—Jig—Interlude—Variations—Rondino

THE ENGLISH WIND PLAYERS

Introit for small orchestra
   and Solo Violin (1925)   *Gerald Finzi*

Solo Violin : ANNE MACNAGHTEN

*Movement for Trumpet
   and Chamber Orchestra (1932)
                        Grace Williams

Solo Trumpet : RICHARD WALTON

**First Concert performance*

</td><td>

ORCHESTRA

1st Violins :—
   ANNE MACNAGHTEN
   WINIFRED SMITH
   KATHLEEN CURRY
   RALPH NICHOLSON

2nd Violins :—
   ELISE DESPREZ
   VIOLET PALMER
   JEAN HOWARD
   JOCELYN GOLDSBROUGH

Violas :—
   BERYL SCAWEN-BLUNT
   NORA WILSON
   PEARL KEELER

'Cellos :—
   MARY GOODCHILD
   URSULA CURRIE
   SUSAN JONES

Double Bass : ADOLF LOTTER

THE ENGLISH WIND PLAYERS

*Flute :—*ARLISS MARIOTT
*Oboe :—*NATHALIE CAINE
*Clarinet :—*STEPHEN WALTERS
*Bassoon :—*CECIL JAMES
Horn : JOHN DENISON

2nd Clarinet :—
   GEOFFREY STURT

Trumpet :—
   RICHARD WALTON

Cor Anglais :—
   SYLVIA SPENCER

2nd Horn :—
   W. BURDETT

Conductor : IRIS LEMARE

</td></tr>
</table>

64 *Lowestoft, c.1934.* Beth. *Photo* C. Wilson, Lowestoft.
65 *London.* Burleigh House, 173 Cromwell Road, s.w.7. *Photo* Jack Phipps.
66 *Burleigh House.* Britten in bed in his room at the private boarding-house where he lodged while a student at the College. His sister Beth, who probably took this photograph, was also a resident. She had a room next to her brother's, which she recalls was very small, with space only for a bed, table and upright piano.

67 *London, 13 December 1933.* Britten informs his parents that he is now an ARCM (Associate of the Royal College of Music).
68 On the beach, 1934. Left to right: Barbara, Mrs Moeran (mother), Mrs Britten, E. J. Moeran (the composer, 1894-1950) and Caesar, the Britten family's dog. Britten's caption: 'Barbara, Mrs Moeran, Mum, Jack Moeran, Caesar on beach July 30'. *Photo* BB.

64 · 65
66

Mr. & Mrs. R. V. Britten,
21. Kirkley Cliff Road,
Lowestoft
Suffolk.

BENJAMIN BRITTEN
A.R.C.M.

Much love

69 *Lowestoft, 9 July 1934.* The programme of a concert at St John's Church. Britten wrote in his diary: 'Quite full – very hot – I play most of the time in just tennis shirt & trousers. We do Schumann conc. – 1st mov. I play slow mov. of Beethoven Appassionata, and 6 small Schönberg pieces, & then with Org. my arr. of F.B.'s 'Moonlight'. Then we struggle thro' Tschaikov. 1st mov. – Mr. Coleman plays Bach E min. pre. & fug., I do L'isle Joyeux [Debussy] and both finish off with Mozart E♭ Symph. Finale – my arr.'

St. John's Church,
Lowestoft.
A
PIANO and ORGAN
RECITAL
by
Mr. Benjamin Britten (Piano)
and
Mr. C. J. R. Coleman (Organ)

Monday, July 9th at 8 p.m.

PROGRAMME.

1. **Fantasia in A minor** . . . *Schumann*
2. **Piano Solos**
3. **"Moonlight" from Suite "The Sea"**
   Frank Bridge arr. B.B.*
   HYMN.
4. **Concerto in B flat minor**
   (1st movement) . . *Tchaikovski*
5. **Prelude and Fugue in E minor**
   for Organ Solo *Bach*
6. **Symphony in E flat (Finale)**
   Mozart arr. B.B.
   **Arranged by permission of the Composer*

GREEN AND CO., PRINTERS, LOWESTOFT.

70 *Lowestoft, December 1934.* Britten's snap of a corner of his own bedroom at the family home. Note the writing desk with a small plaster bust of Beethoven on it. This photograph, as well as No.71, was taken on Britten's return from what he described as his 'European tour' – visits with his mother to Switzerland (Basel), Austria (Salzburg and Vienna), Germany (Munich) and France (Paris), in October and November 1934. *Photo* BB.

71 *Lowestoft, December 1934.* The view of the beach from Britten's bedroom at 21 Kirkley Cliff Road. Britten's caption: 'Back at Lowestoft December 1934'. *Photo* BB.

72 Clive House School, Prestatyn, N. Wales, 1934. This was the school of which Britten's brother, Robert, was headmaster. It was for him and the boys of Clive House that Britten wrote *Friday Afternoons*, Op.7 (1933-5), his twelve children's songs with piano. Britten's caption: 'Clive House School'. *Photo* BB.

73 *Lowestoft, 16 May 1935.* Mrs Britten and Aunt Jane Hockey (the wife of Mrs Britten's brother, William).

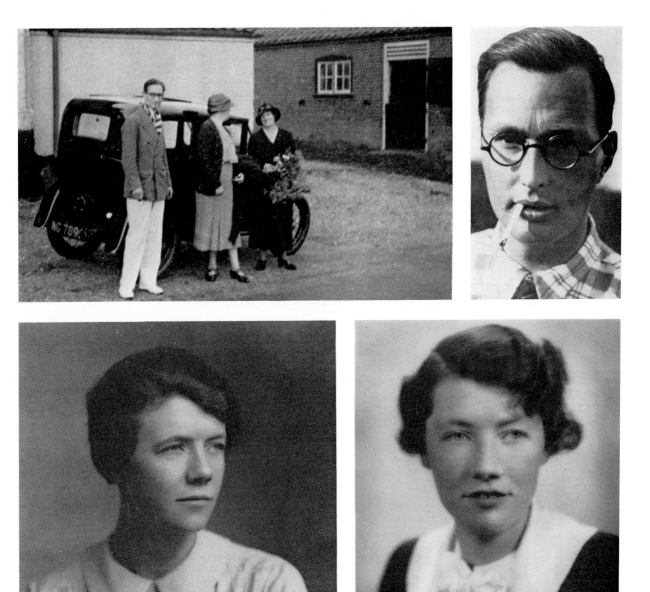

74 *Outside the Gull Inn, Norwich?, 7 September 1934.* Left to right: Henry Boys, the critic and teacher (*b.* 1910) to whom Britten dedicated his Violin Concerto, Op.15; Audrey Alston, Britten's viola teacher from the time he was ten, who had introduced Britten to Frank Bridge; and Mrs Britten. Britten dedicated his *Simple Symphony*, Op.4 (1933-4), to Audrey Alston. (*See No.214* where Henry Boys is listed among the Musical Assistants of the English Opera Group.) *Photo BB.*

75 Eric Walter White (*b.* 1905) in the early 1930s. It was about this time that he first made Britten's acquaintance. He was to publish his first book on Britten – the first major study of the composer – in 1948.
76 *London.* A portrait of Barbara. *Photo Elliott & Fry.*
77 *London.* A portrait of Beth. This probably belongs to the period when she was living in the same boarding-house as her brother, then a student at the College. (*See No.66.*) *Photo Hughes Studios, London.*

National Programme

MARCH 13   **FRIDAY**

DROITWICH	LONDON	WEST	NORTH	
200 kc/s 1,500 m.	1,149 kc/s 261.1 m.	1,149 kc/s 261.1 m.	1,149 kc/s 261.1 m.	National programme continued overleaf

Ⓓ *Programmes marked thus will be radiated by Droitwich, but not by any other National transmitter shown in the heading above.*

10.15 THE DAILY SERVICE
Ⓓ   From page 24 of 'When Two or Three'

Ⓓ   *Time Signal, Greenwich, at 10.30*

10.30 · Weather Forecast
Ⓓ   for Farmers and Shipping

10.45 Children Yesterday and
······—Today—1
······By a Doctor

11.0   FREDRIC BAYCO
at the Organ of the Dominion Theatre, Tottenham Court Road
Overture, Orpheus in the Underworld...........*Offenbach*
Bird on the Wing............*Grosz*
Jack in the Box............*Myers*
Georgia's Rockin' Chair......*Fisher*
Pastoral Scene............*Curzon*
Selection, Thanks a Million
Kahn and Johnston

11.30 FOR THE SCHOOLS
Music and Movement for Very Young Children
ANN DRIVER

11.50 THE RUTLAND SQUARE AND
·· NEW VICTORIA ORCHESTRA
Directed by NORMAN AUSTIN
Relayed from
the New Victoria Cinema, Edinburgh
The Chimney Sweeper............*Rust*
Smilin' through............*Penn*
Fantasia, The Shamrock arr. *Myddleton*
In a Little English Inn............*Coslow*
Love Dance (Madame Sherry) *Hoschna*
Many Happy Returns of the Day
Henry Hall
Fantasia, Sweethearts of Yesterday
arr. *Henry Hall*

12.30   THE B B C
DANCE ORCHESTRA
Directed by HENRY HALL

1.15 Friday Midday Concert
Under the direction of JOHAN HOCK
Relayed from Queen's College
Chambers Lecture Hall, Birmingham
THE BIRMINGHAM PHILHARMONIC
STRING ORCHESTRA
Leader, NORRIS STANLEY
Conductor, JOHAN HOCK
DORIS LANGHAM SMITH (violin)

DORIS LANGHAM SMITH AND ORCHESTRA
Violin Concerto No. 4, in D (K.218)
Mozart
1. Allegro ; 2. Andante grazioso ;
3. Rondeau ; Andante grazioso ;
4. Allegro ma non troppo

ORCHESTRA
Fantasiestücke (Fantasies), Op. 73
Schumann, arr. Brown
1. Con tenerezza ed espressivo ;
2. Allegro con grazia ; 3. Impetuoso
e con fuoco

Time Signal, Greenwich, at 2.0

2.0   Interlude

2.5   FOR THE SCHOOLS
Travel Talk
Southern Europe—8
'The Dalmatian Coast'
FANNY FOSTER

2.25   Interlude

2.30   Music
Course 2, Senior Concert Lesson 4
'Variation Form (b) and the Bassoon'
THOMAS ARMSTRONG, D.Mus.

3.0   Friday Story
Under the direction of
FRANK ROSCOE

SCOTT GODDARD AT THE ALBERT HALL
when he described the scene at last year's Royal Command Concert of British Music. This afternoon at 3.35 he is talking to Sixth Forms on the pleasure of music.

3.15   Friday Talk
Under the direction of
FRANK ROSCOE

3.30   Interval

3.35 Talk for Sixth Forms
'The Arts—2, The Pleasure of Music'
SCOTT GODDARD
(with illustrations)

Scott Goddard is second musical critic of *The Morning Post*. He began his musical career as a chorister at the Temple Church under Sir Walford Davies, and later went to the Royal College of Music, studying composition under Sir Charles Stanford and Charles Wood, organ under Sir Walter Parratt and Sir Walter Alcock, piano under Herbert Sharpe, and conducting under Adrian Boult. For six years he was music master at Leighton Park School, Reading, and then in 1925 became assistant musical critic of *The Observer* until 1929 when he joined the musical staff of *The Morning Post*.

Mr. Goddard frequently appears before the microphone, chiefly in connection with the introductory talks for the BBC Symphony Concerts. He is now to give two talks ; The Pleasure of Music', and a sequel to it entitled 'The Effects of Music'. In this afternoon's talk, 'The Pleasure of Music', he will discuss how people take their music : in the form of a relaxation as they might take a hot bath, or as a kind of bracing tonic in the same way that they might walk across the Downs in a keen wind. Which of these two approaches secures the most from music ? Can music be fully enjoyed just by passive listening, or should the intellect be made to reinforce the ear ?

3.55   Interval

4.0   THE B B C
MIDLAND ORCHESTRA
Leader, ALFRED CAVE
Conducted by LESLIE HEWARD
Overture, Il Seraglio............*Mozart*
La Procession nocturne (The Procession at Night) ....*Rabaud*
Symphony in G minor............*Lalo*
1. Andante—Allegro non troppo ;
2. Vivace ; 3. Adagio ; 4. Allegro
Overture, Cockaigne............*Elgar*

Lalo's Symphony in G minor is dedicated to his friend Charles Lamoureux, the founder of the famous Concerts Lamoureux, which are still a feature of Parisian musical life. It was first performed at one of these concerts, with Lamoureux conducting, on February 13, 1887, and was very favourably received. The Symphony is in four movements : an opening Allegro non troppo with a clear-cut rhythm built

---

BENJAMIN BRITTEN
(left) and
ANTONIO BROSA

who play together in the recital tonight at 10.20.

The programme will include Britten's new suite for violin and pianoforte.

10.20   A Recital
SOPHIE WYSS (soprano)
ANTONIO BROSA (violin)
BENJAMIN BRITTEN (pianoforte)

ANTONIO BROSA AND BENJAMIN BRITTEN
Sonata in G, Op. 30, No. 3..*Beethoven*
1. Allegro assai ; 2. Tempo di minuetto, ma molto moderato e grazioso ;
3. Allegro vivace

10.40 SOPHIE WYSS
Ich ging mit Lust durch einen ⎫
grünen Wald   ⎪
Phantasie   ⎬ *Mahler*
Um schlimme Kinder artig   ⎪
zu machen   ⎭
The Birds ....*Britten*
Daphne   ⎫
Through gilded Trellis ⎭ ····· *Walton*

10.55 ANTONIO BROSA AND BENJAMIN
BRITTEN

Suite for Violin and Pianoforte,
Op. 6 ....*Britten*
1. Introduction ; 2. March ; 3. Moto
perpetuo ; 4. Lullaby ; 5. Waltz

(First performance of complete work)

Benjamin Britten's Suite for violin and piano was begun in Vienna in November, 1934, and completed in London in June, 1935. The violin part affords the soloist plenty of opportunities for a display of virtuosity, and the idiom throughout is distinctly 'modern'. The work is among those chosen for performance at the forthcoming International Contemporary Music Festival in Barcelona.

11.15-12.0 Ⓓ DANCE MUSIC
BILLY COTTON AND HIS BAND

Ⓓ   *Time Signal, Greenwich, at 11.30*

---

78 The *Radio Times*, 6 March 1936. On 13 March at 10.20 p.m. on the National Programme Britten and Brosa gave the first complete performance of the violin and piano Suite, Op.6, which they were to play in Barcelona on 21 April. (*See No.84.*) The prominence given to this recital, in which Sophie Wyss also took part, is evidence of the youthful composer's growing reputation. Note Britten's role as accompanist and the songs by Mahler and Walton.

79-81 *London?, c.1935-6.* Three studies of Britten by Enid Slater (the wife of Montagu Slater, the novelist, poet and playwright, and librettist of *Peter Grimes*). Britten was later to dedicate his *Ballad of Heroes*, Op.14 – texts by W.H. Auden and Randall Swingler, first performed at Queen's Hall on 5 May 1939 as part of a Festival of 'Music for the People' – to Montagu and Enid Slater.

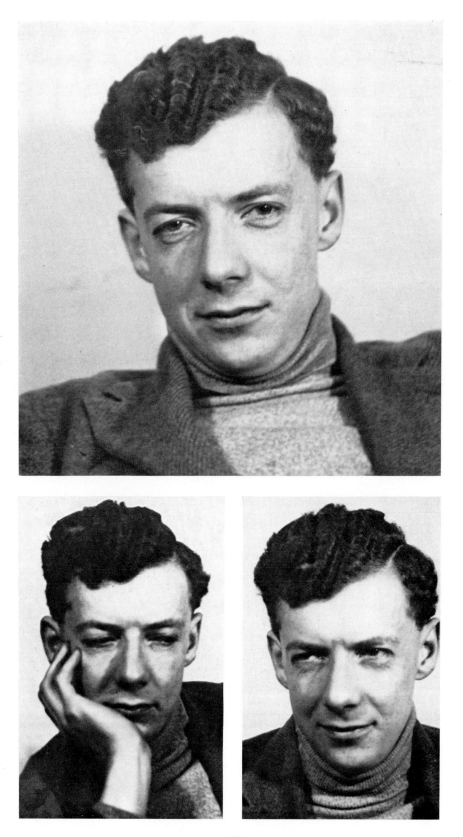

82 *Barcelona, April 1936.* André Mangeot (1883-1970), carrying a violin case, with Julian Herbage and his wife. During the 1920s, Christopher Isherwood was Mangeot's secretary. His employer appears as Cheuvet in Isherwood's autobiographical *Lions and Shadows* (1938), which includes an extended account of life with the Cheuvet family as seen through Isherwood's eyes. Mangeot rendered distinguished service to chamber music (the International String Quartet) and was an early editor and performer of Purcell's *Fantasies.* It was Mangeot and his ensemble who gave a broadcast performance of Britten's unpublished *Phantasy String Quintet* on 17 February 1933, composed in 1932. This had been first performed on 12 December 1932 at a Macnaghten-Lemare concert at the Ballet Club. (*See also No.63.*) *Photo* BB.

83 *Barcelona, April 1936.* Left to right: Jack Gordon, Dorothy Wadham, Peter Burra and Lennox Berkeley. The International Society for Contemporary Music (ISCM) Festival of 1936 was held in Barcelona where, on 21 April, Britten and Antonio Brosa performed the Suite, Op.6. From this trip to Barcelona emerged *Mont Juic,*

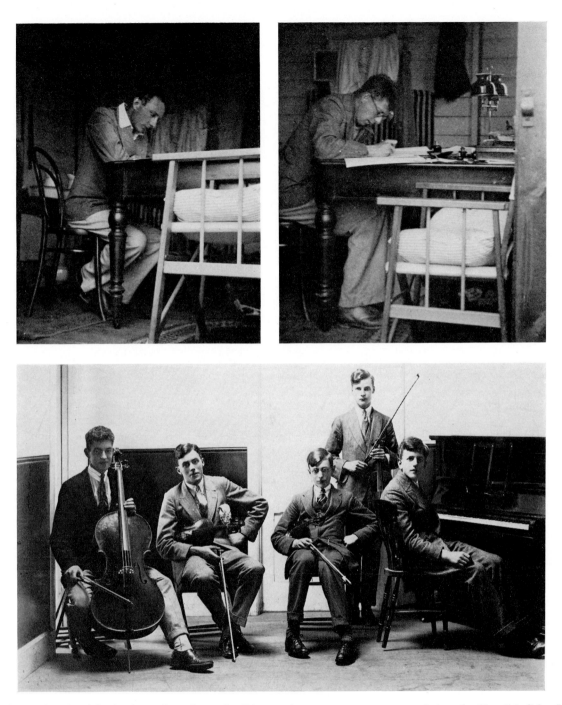

Op.12 (1937), the suite of Catalan dances for orchestra that Britten wrote with Lennox Berkeley and dedicated to the memory of Peter Burra (*see No.87*) who died in an air accident near Reading in April 1937. Britten had known him for just over a year. *Photo* BB.

84 *Barcelona, April 1936.* The Brosa family. Antonio, the fiddler, is on the far right, Peggy his wife, on the far left. *Photo* BB.

85-6 *Crantock, July-August 1936.* Britten went on a working holiday to Cornwall and lived in a chalet in the grounds of the house of Miss Ethel Nettleship. He was joined by Lennox Berkeley and together the two young composers worked at the *Mont Juic* Suite. Left: Lennox Berkeley (to whom the Piano Concerto was to be dedicated), snapped by Britten. Right: Britten, snapped by Berkeley. Britten's caption: 'The composers at work'. *Photo* BB.

87 *Music Room, Lancing College, Sussex, probably 1927.* The Lancing Symphony Orchestra. The violinist standing at the back of the group is Peter Burra (*see No.83*) and the boy at the piano is Peter Pears. The other players on this occasion were (left to right): Michael Richardson, Reginald James and J. F. Rivers-Moore.

88 *Crantock, July 1936.* During this same period (*see Nos. 85 and 86*) Britten was composing his first orchestral song-cycle, *Our Hunting Fathers*, Op.8. In this snap, he is showing the MS of the work to Sophie Wyss, the soprano, who was to give the first performance of the work at the Norwich Festival on 25 September 1936. (She was later to give the first performances of *On this Island*, Op.11, and *Les Illuminations*, Op.18.) Britten's caption: 'Self and Sophie looking at 'Hunting Fathers'.'

89 *Epsom, 1936.* The Sunday before Derby day. Sophie Wyss in the centre, wearing the fur. Britten's caption: 'Arnolds I & II Gyde & Sophie Wyss at Epsom'. (Arnold Gyde was Sophie's husband. Their son was also named Arnold.) *Photo* BB.

90 Montagu Slater (1902-1956). (*See caption to Nos. 79-81.*) Britten composed a setting of a poem by Montagu Slater in 1937 – 'Mother Comfort', one of Two Ballads for two voices and piano. *Photo* Enid Slater.

91 *Stay Down Miner.* A play by Montagu Slater which was produced by the Left Theatre in London in 1936 and for which Britten wrote the incidental music. The 'Wind Song', shown here in Britten's MS, was placed in Act I, Scene 2. Note the scoring for solo voice and

Wind song

91

CENSOR HOLDS UP PEACE FILM

Licence Withheld Until It Has Been Submitted to War Office

THREE-MINUTE APPEAL TO REASON

From our London Staff

FLEET STREET, TUESDAY.

A recent action of the British Board of Film Censors seems likely to arouse considerable criticism in the near future.

A short film, lasting only three minutes, has been made in which the people of Britain are invited to write to their members of Parliament and demand "Peace by reason." The board is withholding a certificate from the film for reasons which, on the face of them, seem to lie quite outside its province.

The film, which is of the ordinary 35mm. inflammable type, is a loosely connected series of short shots with a commentary. It begins with a voice which says: "£2,000,000,000 a year spent on armaments." Shots of aeroplanes, exploding bombs, artillery, tanks, and marching infantry follow in order, while at intervals voices say: "There is no defence against air attack." A mother is shown putting a gas-mask on her child, while voices say in turn: "Gas burns," "Gas blinds," "Gas chokes," "Gas paralyses."

AN APPEAL TO COMMON SENSE

Another voice reminds us that "for the last fifteen years Great Britain has spent £260 a minute, day and night, on armaments." A Union Jack is shown, and across it appears the legend "Make this the symbol of peace." A young working man, a housewife, an ex-soldier, and a professional man in turn give their views on the peace problem in quite general terms, saying that things are just the same as they were before the last war and asking why the Governments cannot get together and settle things. The film ends with the slogans "Demand peace by reason" and "Write to your M.P."

The treatment of the subject throughout is moderate. It suggests the horror and futility of war without hysteria or gruesome detail; it makes no criticism of any person, party, or country; and takes no political line other than the widest one that the nations should negotiate peace instead of fighting for it. To the journalists who saw it privately shown this afternoon it seemed merely an innocuous appeal to common sense. Nevertheless, an effort is being made to prevent its public exhibition.

PROBABLE DELAY

The film was submitted to the film censor in the ordinary way, and the publishers were notified that "exception has been taken by the examiners" to it. From subsequent discussion it appears that the censor regards the film as controversial, but that he will license it if, after submitting it to the War Office, he does not find that parts of it (the shots of artillery and tanks, presumably) are the property of the War Office. The producers say that all the war material in the film has been taken from other commercial films, all of which have been licensed by the censor. The practical result, however, is that the film will be submitted to the War Office, and will probably be held up for a number of weeks, with the result that it will lose a good deal of its topical aptness.

FREE EXHIBITION

The interesting thing is that apparently the War Office did not take the initiative in demanding to see whether its property had been stolen. Nor is it easy to see what grounds for complaint the censor could find in the film if he was acting within his ordinary terms of reference. There is nothing in it which remotely resembles the obscene, blasphemous, or politically provocative. Nor is it a film to which the trade—and the Board of Film Censors is, of course, purely a trade institution—could reasonably take exception. It is true that it is offered free to exhibitors, but it lasts for only three minutes, and so can hardly prevent another film from being rented.

But the censor, it appears, is solicitous for the safety of War Office property. Malicious persons have already been heard to say that the film may to some extent counteract the War Office's appeal for recruits, in connection with which they themselves are about to produce a film.

QUESTION FOR WATCH COMMITTEES

To-day's show was attended by Mr. H. G. Wells, who, though he was sceptical about the merits of the film, said that it was outrageous that it should be suppressed. If the censor's certificate is withheld it is, of course, still open to watch committees to license it for exhibition in their areas. Many cinema managers have already applied to show the film, and the League of Nations Union has circulated its members in each of its 3,000 branches with leaflets informing them about it.

The film has been made by Freenat, the League of Nations Union film unit, and is being distributed by Dofil, Ltd. It has been produced by a number of men prominent in the commercial film industry who wish to remain anonymous, and the initiative came from them and not from the League of Nations Union. Being an inflammable film, it cannot be shown except in a hall which conforms with the Home Office safety regulations.

---

wordless chorus – all male voices – which includes an unusually elaborate form of humming.

92 *London.* In 1936 Britten wrote the music for a short film, *Peace of Britain* (Strand Films), directed by Paul Rotha, which, if not strictly a pacifist document, certainly pleaded a pacifist point of view. When the moment for its release came, there was a clumsy attempt by official-dom to suppress it. Britten writes thus in his diary on 8 April: 'The fuss caused by the Censor not passing that little Rotha Peace film is colossal. ½ centre pages of Herald & News Chronicle, & Manchester Guardian – B.B.C. News twice. Never has a film had such good publicity.' We reproduce the article which appeared in the *Manchester Guardian* of 8 April 1936. The film is further evidence of Britten's involvement in the pacifist cause – a lifelong preoccupation.

93 *The World of the Spirit.* This was a BBC radio feature (5 June 1938), for which Britten composed a substantial choral and orchestral score (81 pages of MS). We reproduce two of the six sections for solo voices which represented the fruits of the Spirit. The text of 6B, from Galatians – 'The fruit of the Spirit is Love, is Peace, is Gentleness' – must have struck a particularly sympathetic response from Britten, involved as he was in these years with the pacifist cause. (6B reminds us indeed of Wingrave's 'Peace' aria.)

Overleaf

94 *Night Mail.* A page from Britten's MS score (note the chamber orchestra and unconventional combination of sandpaper and wind-machine) for the famous documentary film, produced by Harry Watt and Basil Wright for the GPO Film Unit in 1936, with verses by W.H. Auden (1907–1973). It was their work for the Unit which brought Auden and Britten together.

95 *Downs School, Colwall, June 1937.* W.H. Auden, the poet (who was teaching at the school), William Coldstream, the painter (b. 1908), and Britten, the composer, as 'The Three Graces'. Coldstream was also a member of the GPO Film Unit and worked on at least three

"NIGHT-MAIL"
End Sequence
1
Commentator
Flute
Oboe
Bassoon
Trumpet
Percussion
Harp
Violin
Viola
'Cello
'Bass
Sand-paper Wind machine
Bis
Side drum
muted ppp
Wind-machine
pp ad lib.
2
sempre ppp
ppp sul ponticello sempre
3
This is the night mail crossing the border,
Bringing the cheque and the postal order.
Letters for the rich, letters for the poor,
The shop at the corner, the girl next door.
ppp sul pont.
A. L. No 10
Printed in England
Com.
Perc.
'Vc.
CB

films in which Britten was involved, *Coal Face*, *The King's Stamp*, and *Negroes* (*God's Chillun*). In *Coal Face* and *Negroes* Auden was also a collaborator.

96 Britten's own snapshot of Christopher Isherwood (*b.* 1904), from the 1930s. He was to work closely with Isherwood during the Group Theatre period and dedicated *On this Island*, Op.11, to him. There was then a long stretch of time when the two men did not often meet. But in 1976, which was the last summer of Britten's life, Isherwood visited him, and recalled the meeting in these words (in *The Guardian*, 30 March 1977): 'Last summer David Hockney, Don Bachardy, and I went for a drive, up to the north of Scotland, and one of the places we stopped off at was Aldeburgh. I knew Ben was ill, but I didn't know how ill he was. Any emotion was bad for him. He was so moved at seeing us again that he could hardly trust himself to speak. The others left us, and Ben and I sat in a room together, not speaking, just holding hands.'

97 *Colwall, June 1937.* Auden, Hedli Anderson (later Mrs Louis MacNeice) and Coldstream. It was for Hedli Anderson that Britten wrote Four Cabaret Songs (unpublished) on texts by Auden. (*See No.103.*)

98 *London. Agamemnon*, a translation of Aeschylus' play by Louis MacNeice, was produced by Rupert Doone for the Group Theatre in 1936 with music by Britten. These are Robert Medley's original costume designs.

99 Doone was also a dancer and choreographer. (He had been a *premier danseur* for Diaghilev.) In this photograph he is dancing in the Group Theatre production of *Timon of Athens* (1935) for which Britten wrote the incidental music. There was a Ballet (No.6) in the first Banquet scene.

100 A portrait (1935) of Rupert Doone (1903-1966), chief producer during the first period (1932-9) of the Group Theatre. Doone was responsible for the productions of the Auden-Isherwood and MacNeice plays for which Britten composed incidental music. (He was, in fact, the Group's musical director and resident composer.)

101 Robert Medley (*b.* 1905), the Group Theatre's chief designer. This photograph shows him painting the safety curtain design which won a prize offered by the Sadler's Wells Society in 1938.

102 *The Ascent of F.6*. Production photograph from 1937. The designer was Robert Medley.

103 *The Ascent of F.6*. For the Group Theatre production in 1937 of the play by W.H. Auden and Christopher Isherwood, Britten wrote the incidental music. The 'Blues', of which we show the first page in Britten's MS, obviously made a great impression. Britten writes in his diary for 26 February 1937, the night of the first per-formance, 'After the show we all have a good party at the theatre & then feeling very cheerful we all sing (all cast & about 20 audience) my blues as well as going thro' most of the music of the play! Then I play & play & play, while the whole cast dances & sings & fools, & gets generally wild.' (Britten later made a version of the *F.6* 'Blues' for Hedli Anderson – 'Funeral Blues', one of the unpublished Cabaret Songs. *See No.97*.)

BLUES
for the court to be cleared
Voices
Cymbal (soft stick)
ppp
pp
Stop all the clocks, cut off the telephone
Prevent the dog from barking
unis
sempre ppp
B. drum
legato
8va bassa

And Lancelot controls them in P.

BENJAMIN BRITTEN

A CATALOGUE OF WORKS

PUBLISHED BY
BOOSEY & HAWKES LTD.
295 REGENT STREET
LONDON, W.1

BENJAMIN BRITTEN

Benjamin Britten was born at Lowestoft, Suffolk, on November 22nd, 1913. He was educated at Gresham's School, Holt, and studied music during his holidays with Frank Bridge, who has been his constant adviser and friend. While still a boy he entered the Royal College of Music, London, working with John Ireland for composition and with Arthur Benjamin for pianoforte.

Among the first of Britten's compositions to attract serious attention were the *Sinfonietta for Chamber Orchestra* and the *Phantasy Quartet for Oboe and Strings*, the latter gaining a place in the programmes of the I.S.C.M. Festival at Florence in 1934. Both were written at the age of nineteen, and now appear in his list of compositions as Op. 1 and 2. His most important subsequent works are the *Suite for Violin and Piano* (I.S.C.M. Barcelona, 1936); a song-cycle for soprano and orchestra entitled *Our Hunting Fathers* (Norwich Triennial Festival, 1936); the *Variations on a theme of Frank Bridge* for string orchestra (I.S.C.M. London, 1938) which, with more than fifty performances in Europe and America have gained for the composer an international reputation; a large-scale *Pianoforte Concerto* (1938); and a choral work with orchestra, *Ballad of Heroes*, written in the spring of 1939. He is at present (summer 1939) working on a song-cycle with string orchestra *Les Illuminations*, and a *Violin Concerto*.

Britten is an unusually versatile musician. In addition to works for the concert hall he has composed music for a considerable number of broadcast plays and films. He has also been actively associated with the theatre, providing something considerably more than a background to plays by several eminent writers, including W. H. Auden (notably *The Ascent of F6*) and J. B. Priestley. Music of a lighter kind also forms part of his output; he enjoys writing it and would like to improve its generally low standard.

Besides his activities as a composer, Britten is a well-equipped pianist and conductor and has appeared in performances of his works both in England and on the Continent. With one so young —this list of works represents the bulk of his output up to the age of twenty-five—it would be difficult to prophesy his eventual position in the world of music. But there can be no doubt that his achievements are already considerable and of a most remarkable nature, and that the description of him by *The Daily Telegraph* as " unquestionably the most brilliant of the younger British composers " is fully justified.

104 *King Arthur*. This was a BBC radio play (23 April 1937; producer, D.G. Bridson) for which Britten wrote the incidental music. We show the opening page, in Britten's MS, of No.XIVA, with its concertante style of virtuoso writing for pairs of woodwind.

105 A catalogue of Britten's published works issued by Boosey & Hawkes in 1939. He had reached agreement to become one of that company's composers on 3 January 1936. Thus began a momentous association which was to last for the next twenty-eight years.

106 A portrait of Ralph Hawkes (1898-1950), the Chairman of Boosey & Hawkes and an influential figure in the young composer's life.

107 The Old Mill at Snape, Suffolk. This was bought by Britten in late 1937, when it had already undergone conversion.

108 *1938 or 1939*. Britten playing darts in a Suffolk pub. *Photo Enid Slater.*

109 The conversion of the Mill during 1933–4.

110 *Snape, Suffolk, January 1940*. The Old Mill. This photograph was sent to Britten and Pears in the USA, probably by sister Beth, to show them their old home under snow. She lived at the Mill with her family while Britten was in the States and while her husband was on war service, and two of her children were born there (one of them, Sally, *see No.383*). She left the Mill in 1946. For a short period after Britten had left for N. America, Lennox Berkeley (*see No.85*) was also

PROMENADE CONCERT
Thursday 18 August 1938

CONDUCTOR: SIR HENRY J. WOOD

OVERTURE The Barber of Seville   *Rossini*

ARIA The Shepherd on the Rock   *Schubert*

CONCERTO No. 1, in D,
    for Pianoforte and Orchestra *Benjamin Britten*
         (*First performance*)

SYMPHONY No. 4, in G   *Dvořák*

INTERVAL OF FIFTEEN MINUTES

SONGS (with Pianoforte)
              (*a*) Muttertändelei }
              (*b*) Heimkehr   }   *Strauss*
              (*c*) Ständchen   }

(*a*) DANCE OF THE SYLPHS   }
(*b*) MINUET OF THE WILL   } (The Damnation } *Berlioz*
          O' THE WISPS   }   of Faust)   }
(*c*) HUNGARIAN MARCH   }

ELISABETH SCHUMANN
Solo Pianoforte : BENJAMIN BRITTEN

Encores cannot be allowed in the First Part of the Programme

In accordance with the requirements of the London County Council:
I. The public may leave at the end of the performance or exhibition by all exit doors, and such doors
must at that time be open.
II. All gangways, corridors, staircases and external passageways intended for exit shall be kept entirely free from obstruction, whether permanent or temporary.
III. Persons shall not be permitted to stand or sit in any of the gangways intersecting the seating or to
sit in any of the other gangways. If standing be permitted in the gangways at the sides and rear of the seating,
it shall be limited to the numbers indicated in the notices exhibited in those positions.

SMOKING PERMITTED

(Except in the portion of the Grand Circle reserved for non-smokers)
ABDULLAS FOR CHOICE

5

briefly and occasionally in residence at the Mill, at the same time as Beth and her family.

111 *London, 1938.* The programme, together with Britten's programme note, for the Promenade Concert at Queen's Hall on 18 August when Britten appeared as soloist in the first performance of his Piano Concerto, Op.13, conducted by Sir Henry Wood.

3. CONCERTO No. 1, in D, for Pianoforte
                    and Orchestra *Benjamin Britten*
    Allegro molto e con brio
    Allegretto, alla valse
    Recitative and Aria—
    Allegro moderato—sempre alla marcia
            (*First performance*)
Solo Pianoforte BENJAMIN BRITTEN

BEGINNING to compose original music at an age when most young people are struggling with pot-hooks in their first efforts at hand-writing, Britten emerged as an astonishingly mature master of his craft while yet in his teens. When he was only twelve he enlisted as a pupil with Frank Bridge, for whom he holds great affection and admiration; pianoforte studies with Harold Samuel, and composition lessons with John Ireland followed in the next few years, and for some time Britten was a Royal College student. But his work has never revealed much influence of outside impulses; from the first it has been strongly marked by an individual certainty of purpose of his own, and his earliest works made it clear that he was a composer with a very sure and confident grasp of his medium. Using the idiom of to-day as naturally as each of us speaks the language amid which he is brought up, his music is without a trace of the self-conscious air with which older men incorporate new manners and methods, grafting it on to traditions acquired or inherited; in a more than usually real sense, it is music of our own time.   D.M.C.

NOTE BY THE COMPOSER

This Pianoforte Concerto in D was written during the first half of this year and finished on the 27th July. It was conceived with the idea of exploiting various important characteristics of the pianoforte, such as its enormous compass, its percussive quality, and its suitability for figuration; so that it is not by any means a Symphony with pianoforte, but rather a bravura Concerto with orchestral accompaniment. In the first and third movements the effect is that of a duel between the orchestra and the soloist. The four movements are simple and direct in form, but a brief description may be found helpful.

Allegro molto e con brio.—The pianoforte starts the first movement with an energetic leaping *motif* which sets the mood for its own side of the argument. This is the principal subject of the movement. The orchestra continues with a subsidiary phrase which reaches an angry climax in the alternation of two not very closely related chords—an idea which has, however, important significance throughout the work. After some discussion the orchestra introduces hesitatingly the second principal subject—a longer flowing tune on the wood-wind. This the pianoforte mocks in brilliant fashion, and the orchestra tries to further its cause, with the tune (*ff largamente*) in the strings. The second section of the movement presents a grimmer aspect of this material. The first

9

subject appears as an *ostinato* growling in the bass, with the orchestra menacing above it. For a moment the tension is relaxed, but a fierce dialogue between bass and pianoforte interrupts, which in its turn dies away in a series of chromatic runs leading directly to the third section (recapitulation). Here a species of compromise (both subjects appearing at the same time) is attempted and worked out at some length, but it is only after the *cadenza* that the pianoforte is finally tamed and plays the second subject softly and tenderly.

Allegretto, alla valse.—The second movement, again in D, is quiet throughout—as if overheard from the next room. The viola solo and clarinet suggest the first tune and the pianoforte adds the chordal *motif* from the first movement as *codetta*. After a slightly more defined repetition, the pianoforte starts a running theme, supported *pp* by waltz-rhythms in the whole orchestra. This grows louder and louder and eventually the first waltz tune returns energetically and *forte*, as if the door has been slightly opened. But it is soon shut again, and to the end of the movement the mood is that of the beginning. The chordal *motif* is used again and again rather ominously.

Recitative and Aria.—The first section of this movement is in the form of a dialogue between the pianoforte and the various solo instruments of the orchestra (in order, oboe, clarinet, bassoon, flute, horn). One by one they hint at a tune, and the pianoforte rather impertinently makes fun of them. Their mood passes from that of sorrow to indignation, and finally in a burst of wrath (the brass *ff* stating the chordal *motif* from the first two movements) the pianoforte is made to see reason, and when the 'cellos start a broad theme, the pianoforte merely accompanies and interrupts no longer. This theme (which has grown from the seeds sown in the recitatives) is continued with increasing warmth, and is finally stated very broadly by the whole orchestra. As a *coda* the pianoforte, now very subdued, continues the figuration used before as an accompaniment.

Allegro moderato—sempre alla marcia.—Suggestions of marching rhythms follow directly from the previous movement, and lead to a series of march tunes, played full of confidence by the pianoforte and then by the orchestra. A somewhat jingoistic dialogue between the brass and the piano is started, but this has not progressed far when a feeling of doubt creeps into the music, and the marching rhythm fades away inconclusively. The violas and 'cellos have a solemn chant which the pianoforte echoes; but this moment of reflection is soon over, and the marching rhythm begins again in earnest. The development is wholly occupied with this element, and the mood becomes more and more tense. Finally, after a series of crashes in the orchestra against a furious running passage in the pianoforte, the chant reappears in agitated form and the music dies away with mutterings from the orchestra. But bass drum and cymbals start the rhythm again. The pianoforte has a short, excited *cadenza*, and the orchestra shouts the march in all its swagger. The feeling of triumph is increased by a *Presto coda*, and the music rushes headlong to its confident finish.

10

112 *New York, Central Park.* Christopher Isherwood and W.H.
Auden, who left England to settle in the USA in January 1939.
Isherwood was to move on to the West Coast, Auden to remain in
New York. For a highly interesting account of the voyage and the
feelings involved in the departure, see Isherwood, *Christopher and
His Kind* (New York, 1976, pp.317ff). This photograph, however,
probably belongs to the summer of 1938, the occasion of Auden's and
Isherwood's first visit to the USA, on their return from their cele-
brated journey to China.

113 *New York, 1941.* Britten and Auden when the rehearsals of
Paul Bunyan were in progress (*see also No.143*). In what was probably
intended as a tribute to Britten on his fiftieth birthday but never

published, Auden wrote: 'I have, alas, no talent for writing memoirs,
for if I had, I would devote a whole chapter to a house in Amityville,
Long Island, the home of Dr William and Elizabeth Mayer, where
Benjamin Britten and Peter Pears stayed in 1939-40; a house which
played an important role in the lives of all three of us. It was during
this period that Britten wrote his first opera, and I my first libretto,
on the subject of an American folk hero, Paul Bunyan. The result,
I'm sorry to say, was a failure, for which I was entirely to blame,
since, at the time, I knew nothing whatsoever about opera or what is
required of a librettist. In consequence, some very lovely music of
Britten's went down the drain, and I must now belatedly make
apologies to my old friend, while wishing him a very happy birthday.'

GRAMERCY 5-1930

George Washington Hotel
Twenty-Third Street and Lexington Avenue
New York City, N. Y.

My dear Mrs Mayer.

Please look at the signature first, and then let me tell you that I ought to have written to you many times since I last saw you 18 months ago. But because I haven't written it doesn't mean that I haven't thought often of you, particularly in the hurricane of September and then through all these recurrent crises that we in Europe have been enduring —

But anyway the important thing is that after nearly two months in Canada in Quebec Province and then in Toronto, I and my friend Benjamin Britten, composer, have just arrived in New York, and I am so looking forward to seeing you again —

Please will you & Michael have lunch or tea with us tomorrow (Friday)? I will ring you up in the morning to see if you can. On Saturday we go into the country near Poughkeepsie until the end of July (except for two nights in New York about the 12th) and for August we go to the sea — I sail for England again on August 26th or so, and shall have a few days in New York then. So I hope to see you a lot —

My love to you all   yours ever Peter Pears.

Edgar Zilsel   July 5, 1939
Lotte Jacobi   July 8, 1939
Mary Murray   July 12, 1939
Catherine Murray   July 12, 1939
Evelyn Casey   Aug. 4, 1939
Ulrica Elizabeth Mayer   "   "
Marie Thea Wittkowann Aug. 6. 1939
[signature] [signature] Aug. 6 1939
Henry G. Knaf — Nelo Knaf Aug. 6 1939
Benjamin Britten   August. 21st 1939
Peter Pears.
Isabelle J. Wengenroth   Aug. 22-39
                                    Blue Point Long Island.
Evelyn Casey   Aug. 23, 1939
Ulrica Elizabeth Mayer   "   "
Arthur Kaufmann   Aug. 27/1939
...ystan Arden   Sept 4th
Colin McPhee   Sept 7.

114 A letter from Peter Pears to Mrs Elizabeth Mayer announcing his arrival, and Britten's, in New York in late June 1939. They had left England in May and travelled first to Canada. The projected return trip to the UK in August was of course never made.

115 *Amityville, Long Island, New York*: a page from the Mayers' Visitors' Book. Pears' and Britten's names appear for the first time on 21 August 1939. On this same page are inscribed the names of the photographer, Lotte Jacobi (8 July: *see Nos. 149–53*), W. H. Auden (4 September) and Colin McPhee (7 September: *see also No.125*).

116 *Amityville*. Stanton Cottage, the Mayers' house in the grounds of the Long Island Home of which Dr William Mayer was medical director.

114 · 115 116

117 *Amityville*. Peter Pears outside Stanton Cottage.

118 *Amityville*. Britten outside Stanton Cottage.

119 *Amityville*. Dr William Mayer (1887-1956) outside his home. He had practised as a psychiatrist in Munich until obliged to emigrate in 1936, when he found employment in the USA. He was later joined by his wife and children.

120 *Amityville*. Mrs Elizabeth Mayer (1884-1970) with Jippy (*see No.122*). She was a passionate lover of the arts, above all of music, and was quick to recognize the exceptional gifts of her English visitors,

who were to stay within the ambit of the remarkable Mayer household until their return to the UK. Mrs Mayer's many skills included translation (where she collaborated with W.H. Auden, another close friend). But it was her understanding and encouraging of artists which was her unique talent and which made her home in Amityville a magnetic centre which drew to it many of the outstanding creative people living in the States in the late 1930s and 1940s. Stanton Cottage was in every sense a home for Britten and Pears, even when they were absent from it. The *Hymn to St Cecilia*, Op.27, to a text by Auden, was dedicated to her.

MY BIRTHDAY !! Nov. 22ⁿᵈ 1959

Aet: 26 y.

Benjamin Britten

Elizabeth Mayer

Wystan Auden

Peter Pears.

Chester Kallman

Beata Mayer

Michael G Mayer

Christopher Mayer

William Mayer

Ulrica Mayer

* chippy Mayer

121 *Amityville, c.1942.* The Mayer family. Left to right: Mrs Mayer, Sgt Michael G. Mayer (son), Dr Mayer, Christopher Mayer (son), Dr Max Wachstein (Beata's first husband, *d.* 1965) and Beata Mayer. (Ulrica Mayer, the second daughter, was away from home at the time this photograph was taken.)
122 The Mayers' Visitors' Book. The entry for Britten's twenty-sixth birthday on 22 November 1939 (similar entries exist for subsequent birthdays). Among the guests were W. H. Auden and his poet friend and collaborator, Chester Kallman. The blot on the right is an imprint of the pad of the Mayer dog Jippy (or Jip), named thus after the dog in Hugh Lofting's Dr Doolittle books. Jippy (*see No.120*) may have been the model for Fido in *Paul Bunyan.* He clearly could not spell.
123 *Jones Beach, Long Island.* Beata, the Mayer daughter who was closest to Britten and Pears. For a time (mostly in 1939-40) she acted as Britten's unofficial secretary and was later employed in the Artists' Bureau of his publishers in New York, Boosey & Hawkes.
124 *Amityville.* Ulrica, Beata's sister.

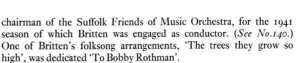

125 *Amityville*. Britten and the Canadian Colin McPhee (1901-1964) outside Stanton Cottage. It was during this period that Britten and McPhee – who was both a composer and an authority on the music of Bali – recorded some of the latter's transcriptions for two pianos of Balinese music. (*See Nos.174 and 176.*)

126 *Jones Beach*. Britten and Pears.

127 *Amityville, 1941?*. Britten with Bobby Rothman, the son of David Rothman, owner of a hardware store at Southold and a regional chairman of the Suffolk Friends of Music Orchestra, for the 1941 season of which Britten was engaged as conductor. (*See No.140.*) One of Britten's folksong arrangements, 'The trees they grow so high', was dedicated 'To Bobby Rothman'.

128 *Amityville*. The Long Island Home. This photograph shows the therapeutic centre where patients could relax. (The L.I. Home was a hospital for the mentally ill.) Britten and Pears gave occasional recitals in the centre or used it for rehearsals.

129 *Chicago, 15 January 1940*. Britten with Albert Goldberg during the rehearsal for the first performance in the USA of the Piano Concerto, in which Britten was soloist.

130 Boyd Neel. It was for Boyd Neel and his String Orchestra that Britten composed his *Variations on a Theme of Frank Bridge*, Op.10, first performed at the Salzburg Festival in August 1937. Neel also conducted the first complete performance of *Les Illuminations* in London in 1939. For him and his orchestra Britten wrote the Prelude and Fugue, Op.29, for 18-part string orchestra, in 1943 after his return from the USA in the previous year.

131 *London, 30 January 1940*. The programme for the first complete performance of *Les Illuminations*, Op.18. (Britten was in the USA at this time.) The work was dedicated to Sophie Wyss. (*See Nos.88-9*.) Performances of two of the songs had been given before Britten finally completed the work as a continuous cycle. 'Being Beauteous' and 'Marine' were heard at the Proms, for example, at Queen's Hall, 17 August 1939, with Sophie Wyss as soloist, conducted by Sir Henry Wood. They appeared in the programme as 'Two Songs with String Orchestra', first London performance. Peter Pears gave the USA première of *Les Illuminations* in New York on 18 May 1941 as part of the ISCM Festival of that year.

132 Barbara. A photograph sent to Britten while he was in America. *Photo* Enid Slater.

LONDON CONTEMPORARY MUSIC CENTRE
(British Section of the International Society for Contemporary Music)

announces its

FIRST ORCHESTRAL CONCERT

AEOLIAN HALL

135, New Bond Street, W.1

on

Tuesday, January 30th, 1940, at 5.30 p.m.

THE BOYD NEEL ORCHESTRA

Conductor : BOYD NEEL

Leader : FREDERICK GRINKE

Soprano :
SOPHIE WYSS

Tickets, tax free : Reserved 5/- ; Unreserved 2/-

From The Aeolian Hall, 135, New Bond Street, W.1. (Phone : Mayfair 6761); the Hon. Secretary, Mrs. H. M. Hart, Hill House, 2 Hill Road, N.W.8 (phone : Maida Vale 1577) from whom all particulars can be obtained.

Each member of the L.C.M.C. is entitled to one free reserved seat. A ticket can be obtained on application to the Hon. Secretary.

(Programme overleaf)

133 *Maine, USA, September 1940.* Britten, Pears and Eugene Goossens, who was then conductor of the Cincinnati Symphony Orchestra. Goossens was staying in Maine, and Britten and Pears arranged to visit him there to discuss 'matters musical', as Britten put it, and the possibility of their making a trip to Cincinnati at Christmas, a trip that finally did not materialize. Britten and Pears had themselves already been in Maine, at the Owl's Head Inn, from 10 to 26 August. It was there that Britten completed work on the *Diversions* for Paul Wittgenstein. (*See No.157.*) After leaving Owl's Head, Britten and Pears travelled to Williamsburg, Mass., where they stayed at the home of Mina Curtiss (*b.* 1896), later to be the editor and translator of Proust's letters and biographer of Bizet, and sister of Lincoln Kirstein (*b.* 1907), the distinguished administrator of American ballet to whom Britten dedicated his *Matinées Musicales*, Op.24. W.H. Auden was also living in Williamsburg at the time, which enabled the collaboration with Britten on *Paul Bunyan* to proceed (and also, according to a letter of Britten's, on the *Hymn to St Cecilia*, Op.27, a very early mention of a project that was only to be completed on the voyage home in 1942). It was towards the end of this Williamsburg stay that Britten and Pears made the side-trip to Maine to see Goossens. They returned to Mina Curtiss's home (Chapelbrook) and, after a final weekend there, made their way back to Amityville. Later in the year they took up residence in Brooklyn Heights.

VIOLIN PASSAGES

EXTRACTED

By

BENJAMIN BRITTEN

and

ANTONIO BROSA

FROM THE WORKS OF THE FOLLOWING
WORLD FAMOUS COMPOSERS

ARNE, T. A.
BACH, J. S.
CORELLI, A
HANDEL, G.
HAYDN, F. J.
MOZART, W. A.

$1.00

BOOSEY & HAWKES, INC.

NEW YORK, U. S. A.

Sole Distributors, U. S. A.
BOOSEY, HAWKES, BELWIN, INC.
43-47 WEST 23rd STREET
NEW YORK CITY

BOOSEY & HAWKES, LTD.
295 Regent Street
London, W. 1

BOOSEY & HAWKES, (CANADA) LTD
10 Shuter Street
Toronto

BOOSEY & HAWKES (AUSTRALIA) PTY., LTD.
National Building, 250 Pitt Street
Sydney
Printed in U. S. A.

134 *New York, 1941.* An almost unknown publication. The title-page of the first volume of what was clearly intended to be a series devoted to difficult violin passages, 'extracted' by Britten and Brosa. As Britten was about to leave for the UK in March 1942 he wrote to Brosa: 'I do hope you don't mind doing the Violin Book, Toni – but in a way it will be a good investment – when we're old and gray it may be nice to have $10 a year to buy candies with – !' A further volume of excerpts (from the nineteenth century) was planned but seems not to have materialized.

135 Antonio Brosa by Marjorie Fass.

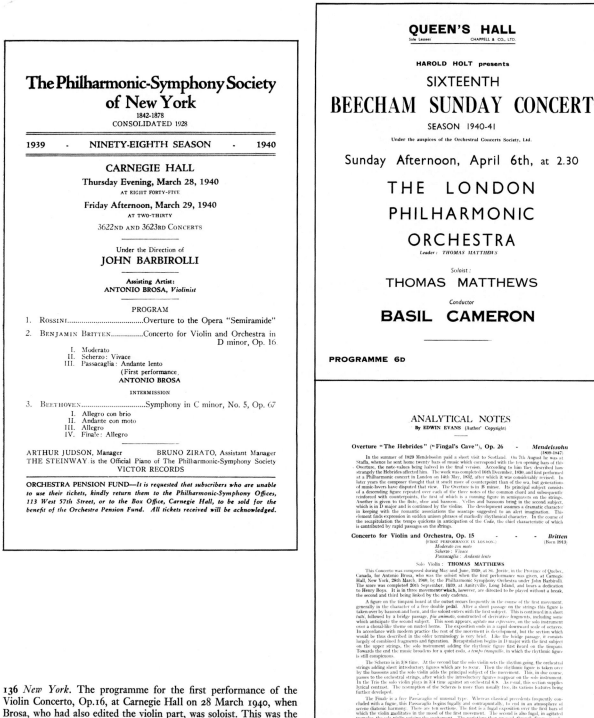

136 *New York.* The programme for the first performance of the Violin Concerto, Op.16, at Carnegie Hall on 28 March 1940, when Brosa, who had also edited the violin part, was soloist. This was the first work Britten completed after his arrival in North America.

137 *London, 1941.* The programme for the London première of the Violin Concerto, just a year after the work's first performance in New York. This London performance took place while Britten was in the USA.

BENJAMIN BRITTEN
Conductor

The Suffolk
Friends of Music Orchestra

Season 1941

BENJAMIN BRITTEN, Conductor

The Suffolk Friends of Music announce with pride the engagement of the noted English composer, pianist and conductor, Benjamin Britten, as their conductor. A graduate of the Royal College of Music, the London Daily Telegraph speaks of him as "unquestionably the most brilliant of the younger British composers." Though he is now but 27 years old, his compositions have been featured by the major festivals of England and the Continent. In the United States, Britten compositions have been performed by Albert Stoessel's Chatauqua Orchestra, Wallenstein's WOR Sinfonietta, and the New York Philharmonic Orchestra, under Barbirolli. Mr. Britten's new "Sinfonia da Requiem" will be played by the New York Philharmonic on March 29 and 30, 1941.

As conductor, Mr. Britten has appeared with the British Broadcasting Company Orchestra, the London Philharmonic and the London Symphony, and also has spent a period as conductor of the English government film project.

A Symphony Orchestra in Suffolk County

The Suffolk Friends of Music Orchestra is composed of three types of players: professional musicians, adult amateurs, and advanced students of high school age. All volunteer their services in the orchestra for the sole reward of establishing in Suffolk a permanent symphony orchestra, sincere in its musical purpose, and aiming high in artistic achievement.

Attracting new players with each rehearsal, the Orchestra numbered forty-five players in December, 1940. Concerts are planned for the months of March and April in Southampton, Riverhead, Port Jefferson and Amityville.

The Musical Advisory Board

The Musical Advisory Board consists of several internationally prominent musicians who indorse the work of the SUFFOLK FRIENDS OF MUSIC OR-

CHESTRA. Some are residents of Suffolk. They are as follows:

DOUGLAS MOORE, Chairman, Head of Music Department of Columbia College, Cutchogue and New York.
NATHALIE BOSHKO, Concert Violinist, Southampton and New York.
VICTOR HARRIS, Composer, East Hampton and New York.
PHILLIP JAMES, Head of Music Department, New York University, Amagansett and New York.
HARWOOD SIMMONS, Director of Columbia University Concert Band and the New York City Symphonic Band.
SIGMUND SPAETH, Author, Lecturer and Composer.

Officers of the Suffolk Friends of Music Orchestra

PRESIDENT .... Jack Van Brederode
HONORARY PRESIDENT .... Jesse Lillywhite
VICE-PRESIDENT & BUSINESS MANAGER ...... Walter Potter
SECRETARY .... Donald Barth, Riverhead, N. Y.
TREASURER .... Milton Samuel, Mattituck, N. Y.
PUBLICITY COMMITTEE ... Howard Lee Koch, Anne Vojvode
LIBRARIANS ... Jack Cushman, Robert Richard, Thomas Stark

REGIONAL CHAIRMEN:
Bellport, Donald Baggs; Bridgehampton, Charles Mockler; Center Moriches, Chester Osborne; East Hampton, Molly Smith; Hampton Bays, John Knapp; Mattituck, Walter Williams; Port Jefferson, Jesse Van Brederode; Riverhead, Howard Hovey; Southampton, Jesse Lillywhite; Southold, David Rothman.

Associate Memberships

The Orchestra has already received several donations from music lovers who have heard of its development. This has led to the establishment of The Associate Members of the Suffolk Friends of Music. In appreciation of this support, a private chamber music recital will be given for these associate members and the regular members of the orchestra at the close of the concert season in May. Featuring prominent soloists, the recital will be held in the new Nathalie Boshko Studio, Artist Colony, Southampton.

The Suffolk Friends of Music Orchestra solicits the Associate Membership of all who are interested in a permanent symphony orchestra in Suffolk County.

138 *New York, c.1940.* Peter Pears. *Photo* E. Nash, New York.
139 *Riverhead, Long Island.* Britten conducting the Suffolk Friends of Music Orchestra in the Canzonetta from his *Soirées Musicales*, Op.9.
140 A leaflet announcing Britten's appointment as conductor of the Suffolk Friends of Music Orchestra, Suffolk County, Long Island, in 1941.
141 *New York, 1941.* The poster for the first performance of *Paul Bunyan. Photo* New York Public Library, Berg Collection.

THE COLUMBIA THEATER ASSOCIATES PRESENT
PAUL BUNYAN
A NEW OPERETTA
IN 2 ACTS
Book by
W. H. AUDEN
Music by
BENJAMIN BRITTEN
THE WEEK OF MAY 5
BRANDER MATTHEWS HALL
420 WEST 117th STREET
EVENINGS AT 8:40 - - - SATURDAY MATINEE AT 2:40
ADMISSION 50¢ OR BY SUBSCRIPTION
BOX OFFICE OPEN DAILY FROM 10 A.M. TO 6 P.M.

142 *New York, c.1941.* A sketch for *Paul Bunyan.* The music is in Britten's hand and, like the diagram below it, seems to be an early attempt at an outline of the 'Blues: Quartet of Defeated' in Act I, Scene 1 (the final version differs from the notation shown here). The text (at the right) is in Auden's hand, a verse for Johnny Inkslinger from the Christmas Party, Act II, Scene 2. *Photo* New York Public Library, Berg Collection.

143 *New York, 1941.* Britten and Auden at the time of the rehearsals for *Paul Bunyan.* (*See also No.113.*)

144 *New York, 5 May 1941.* The programme for the first performance of *Paul Bunyan.* It contains (p.4) some revealing thoughts about the work by the poet and composer.

THE COLUMBIA THEATER ASSOCIATES

OF COLUMBIA UNIVERSITY

present

PAUL BUNYAN

by W. H. Auden and Benjamin Britten

WITH THE CO-OPERATION OF

The Columbia University Department of Music

AND A CHORUS FROM

The New York Schola Cantorum

Hugh Ross, Conductor

BRANDER MATTHEWS HALL

WEEK OF MAY 5, 1941

PAUL BUNYAN

Book by W. H. Auden; Music by Benjamin Britten

Directed by Milton Smith; Musical Director – Hugh Ross

CHARACTERS

In the Prologue

Old Trees	CHORUS
Young Trees	ELLEN HUFFMASTER, JANE WEAVER, MARLOWE JONES, BEN CARPENS
Three Wild Geese	HARRIET GREENE, AUGUSTA DORN, PAULINE KLEINHESSELINK

In the Interludes

Narrator	MORDECAI BAUMAN

In the Play

The Voice of Paul Bunyan	MILTON WARCHOFF
Cross Crosshaulson	WALTER GRAF
John Shears	LEONARD STOCKER
Sam Sharkey	CLIFFORD JACKSON
Ben Benny	EUGENE BONHAM
Jen Jenson	ERNEST HOLCOMBE
Pete Peterson	LEWIS PIERCE
Andy Anderson	BEN CARPENS
Other Lumberjacks	ALAN ADAIR, ELMER BARBER, ARNOLD JAFFE, MARLOWE JONES, CHARLES SNITOW, ROBERT ZELLER, W. FREDRIC PLETTE, THOMAS FLYNN, JOSEPH HARROW
Western Union Boy	HENRY BAUMAN
Hel Helsen	BLISS WOODWARD
Johnny Inkslinger	WILLIAM HESS
Fido	PAULINE KLEINHESSELINK
Moppet	HARRIET GREENE
Poppet	AUGUSTA DORN
The Defeated	BEN CARPENS, EUGENE BONHAM, ADELAIDE VAN WEY, ERNEST HOLCOMBE

Slim	CHARLES CAMMOCK
Tiny	HELEN MARSHALL
The Film Stars and Models	ELEANOR HUTCHINGS, ELLEN HUFFMASTER, BEN CARPENS, LEWIS PIERCE
Frontier Women	MARIE BELLEJEAU, ELOISE CALINGER, IRMA COMMANDAY, ALICE GERSTZ DUSCHAK, MARIAN EDWARDS, ELIZABETH FLYNN, ROSE HARRIS, ETHEL MADSEN, JEAN PHILLIPS, EVELYN RAY, IRMA SCHOCKEN, ADELAIDE VAN WEY, JANE WEAVER, IDA WEIRICH, MARJORIE WILLIAMSON

Scene: A Grove in a Western Forest

Prologue . . . Night

Act I, Scene 1. A spring morning.
   Scene 2. Summer.

Intermission — Ten Minutes

Act II, Scene 1. Autumn.
   Scene 2. Christmas.

Settings designed by John W. Love, and built and painted by members of the play production classes under Mr. Love's supervision.

Lighting designed and executed by Stuart Machlin.

Makeup supervised by Kenneth Buckridge.

This production is made possible by a grant from the Alice M. Ditson Fund.

"PAUL BUNYAN" is the first operatic collaboration between Mr. W. H. Auden, one of the best-known young English poets, and Mr. Benjamin Britten, one of the most distinguished young English composers. The Columbia Theater Associates welcome the opportunity to present the world premiere of this interesting composition. The authors describe their work as a choral operetta, ". . . with many small parts rather than a few star roles." They explain that they conceive of Paul Bunyan, the giant hero of the Lumbermen, and one of the many mythical figures who appeared in American folklore during the Pioneer period, as ". . . . a projection of the collective state of mind of a people whose tasks were primarily the physical mastery of nature. This operetta presents in a compressed fairy-story form the development of the continent from a virgin forest before the birth of Paul Bunyan to settlement and cultivation when Paul Bunyan says goodbye because he is no longer needed, i.e., the human task is now a different one, of how to live well in a country that the pioneers have made it possible to live in."

MR. W. H. AUDEN has published five volumes of poems, two travel books, and two plays: "The Dog Beneath the Skin" and "The Ascent of F6." He has written extensively for radio, often in collaboration with Mr. Britten.

MR. BENJAMIN BRITTEN is a distinguished conductor and a productive composer with much work to his credit. In the course of 1940 he wrote, in addition to "Paul Bunyan," a Symphony, a Piano Concerto, a Rondo for two Pianos, incidental music for two plays, a Piano Sonatina, settings for eight Michel Angelo Sonnets, and other small pieces. Many of these compositions have already had public performances. His Symphony, "Sinfonia da Requiem," was played by the New York Philharmonic Orchestra on March 30, 1941.

IN PRESENTING "PAUL BUNYAN," The Columbia Theater Associates hope that several precedents are being established. There are a number of ways in which the production is a "first." Not only is it the first production of the first operetta of the librettist and the composer, but it is also the first formal collaboration between the Associates and the Columbia University Department of Music. In addition, this is the first time we have had the assistance of singers from that well-known choral group, The New York Schola Cantorum, and the first time we have had a music director for one of our operas who was not a member of the Columbia staff. We are glad to welcome, for what we hope will be only the first of many times, the distinguished Conductor of the Schola Cantorum, Mr. Hugh Ross.

THE LEAGUE OF COMPOSERS is taking, for the first time, a pre-view of one of our productions in order to encourage the presenting of original operettas in universities, and has commissioned several works for next year. The League hopes in this way to establish a "Composers' Theater," and to encourage the composition and the performance of new American operas in American universities. We hope, therefore, that this will be only the first of a long series of new operas and operettas given throughout the country under the auspices of the League. Finally, with this production of "Paul Bunyan," we bring to a close our first season in our new theater, Brander Matthews Hall.

THE COLUMBIA THEATER ASSOCIATES is an affiliation of the acting groups of the University. It grows directly out of the work of the Morningside Players, who were organized in 1916 to present original and experimental productions, and The Columbia Laboratory Players, who were organized in 1922 to present revivals of Shakespearian and other early English and American plays. Since 1927, a constant program of five or six productions a season has been maintained in Earl Hall. This season we have made six productions. All present and past members of the University are invited to take an active part in our work.

NEXT SEASON we plan to present six or seven productions. Among them will be two or three new scripts, one or two revivals, and a new operetta. You are invited to subscribe. Subscribers receive six ticket coupons for $2.00, and are advised by mail of coming productions. The coupons may be exchanged for reserved seats in any combination. Columbia University students may subscribe for $1.00 upon presentation of Bursar's receipt.

REQUEST FOR SUBSCRIPTION BLANK

Columbia Theater Associates
Brander Matthews Hall
420 West 117th Street
New York City

Please send me information and a subscription blank for the season of 1941-42.

NAME (Please print)..

ADDRESS ....

....

PRODUCTION STAFF FOR "PAUL BUNYAN"

Company Manager	LOREN CROSTEN
Assistant Directors	ROBERT VAMBERY, LOUISE GIFFORD
Stage Manager	VICTOR KOMOW
Assistant Stage Managers	GRETCHEN BURKHALTER, W. FREDRIC PLETTE, THOMAS FLYNN
Property Manager	HARRIET WITTSTEIN
Assistant Property Managers	RUTHANN SAMPSON, ROSE SLATER
Sound Technician	PROSPER INVERNIZZI
Electrician	STUART MACHLIN
House Manager	H. HOLT RIDDLEBERGER

COLUMBIA THEATER ASSOCIATES

EXECUTIVE COMMITTEE
Milton Smith, Chairman

For The Morningside Players
EDWIN S. FULCOMER
HATCHER HUGHES
MARY LOU PLUGGE
BLISS WOODWARD

For The Columbia Laboratory Players
HAROLD CLAUSEN
GERTRUDE KELLER
EDWARD MAMMEN

For The Columbia College Players
BRUCE CARTER
EVALD GASSTROM
BENJAMIN HUBBARD
JACK ROSEN

For The Julliard Institute Opera Players
LUCIA DUNHAM
CHARLES RASELY
MILTON WARCHOFF

145 *Escondido, California, 1941*. Britten and Pears with the two-piano team, Ethel Bartlett and Rae Robertson, at their home in California. It was for this duo that Britten wrote his *Introduction and Rondo alla Burlesca*, Op.23, No.1 (1940); the *Mazurka Elegiaca*, Op.23, No.2 (1941), for two pianos; and the *Scottish Ballad*, Op.26 (1941), for two pianos and orchestra. This last work was given its première at Cincinnati on 28 November 1941 with Goossens conducting (*see No.133*) and Bartlett and Robertson as soloists. *Photo* John Mundy Jnr.

146-8 *Escondido, Summer 1941*. Britten.
149 *Amityville, 29 December 1941*. Britten and Pears at the piano at Stanton Cottage. *Photo* Lotte Jacobi.
150 *Amityville, 29 December 1941*. Mrs Mayer, Pears and Britten. Mrs Mayer (*see No.120*) had in her youth studied at the Royal Conservatory of Music, Stuttgart, when her ambition was to become a professional pianist. *Photo* Lotte Jacobi.
151 *Amityville, 29 December 1941*. Britten. *Photo* Lotte Jacobi.

152 *Amityville, 29 December 1941*. Britten. *Photo* Lotte Jacobi.
153 *Amityville, 29 December 1941*. Britten's hands. *Photo* Lotte Jacobi.
Overleaf
154 The Music Library of the New York Public Library: Britten's and Pears' library cards for 1941-2. Note the address: 7 Middagh Street, Brooklyn Heights. This old brownstone house was owned by George Davis, then fiction editor of *Harper's Bazaar* and a friend of Auden and Isherwood. (He was later to marry Kurt Weill's widow, Lotte Lenya.) Auden acted as house 'father' and among the residents at various times were Carson McCullers, Gypsy Rose Lee, Golo

Mann, Louis MacNeice, Paul Bowles, Richard Wright, Chester Kallman, Salvador and Gala Dali, Janet Flanner, Oliver Smith (*see No. 206*) – and Britten and Pears, who moved in to Middagh Street on their return to New York from Maine in November 1940. (*See No.133*.) They did not much care in the end for the somewhat raffish character of Middagh Street and in the summer of 1941 left for California. (*See Nos.145-8*.) The exotic life of this Brooklyn household has been thoroughly documented by Virginia Spencer Carr in her biography of Carson McCullers (New York, 1976, Chapter 7).
155 'In the streets of New York . . .' (*Paul Bunyan*, Act I), Brooklyn Heights, *c*.1940. Pears and Britten.

156 *Boston, 2 January 1942*. Britten with Serge Koussevitzky (1874–1951), who had conducted with the Boston Symphony a performance of the *Sinfonia da Requiem*, Op.20. It was Koussevitzky who commissioned *Peter Grimes*, Op.33 (1945), to be dedicated to the memory of his wife Natalie who had recently died. (*See also No.207*.)

157 Britten with Paul Wittgenstein, the pianist, who commissioned the *Diversions*, Op.21, for piano (left hand) and orchestra. The first performance was given by the Philadelphia Orchestra under Eugène Ormandy on 16 January 1942. The work was completed in Maine in the summer of 1940. (*See No.133*.)

158 *Boston, 1942*. Koussevitzky, with the inscription: 'to my dear / Benjamin Britten / with admiration and warm wishes'.

159 The MS *Axel Johnson*, on which Britten and Pears returned to the UK in 1942. They boarded the boat at New York on 16 March 1942 (an event recorded in Mrs Mayer's diary: 'I bring B. and P. to the boat 3 p.m.' On the margin is written: 'The Ides of March').

After waiting several days in New York and stopping at other places on its journey up the coast, the boat reached Boston on 25 March; but the actual crossing was made from the port of Halifax, Nova Scotia. The total journey took, it seems, nearly five weeks, but only twelve days of these were spent on the Atlantic crossing. Mrs Mayer's diary for 17 April reads: 'Cable from Ben and Peter'. This, then, must have been the date on which they arrived back in the UK. Britten was busy composing throughout the voyage the *Hymn to St Cecilia* and *A Ceremony of Carols*, Op.28 – the former is inscribed 'At sea, M.S. Axel Johnson, 2 April 1942' and the latter 'At sea, M.S. Axel Johnson, Spring 1942'. Pears wrote to Mrs Mayer that the N.Y. Customs had relieved Britten of his MSS, whereupon Britten 'wrote [the *Hymn*] all out again and finished it (very lovely!) and also wrote 7 Christmas Carols for women's [*sic*] voices and Harp'. On arrival, Britten's MSS were yet again temporarily confiscated, this time by the English authorities. Among the MSS that were impounded in New York (though these were eventually returned to the composer) was a sketch for a Clarinet Concerto, destined for Benny Goodman. This was a project to which Britten had given some thought but, once back in the UK, he did not return to it.

NATIONAL GALLERY CONCERTS

PETER PEARS (*Tenor*)

BENJAMIN BRITTEN (*Pianoforte*)

Programme

I

SONG CYCLE, " DICHTERLIEBE," OP. 48 (POET'S LOVE)   *Schumann*

Im wunderschönen Monat Mai (The Lovely month of May)
Aus meinen Thränen spriessen (Each tear I shed in sorrow)
Die Rose, die Lilie, die Taube (The Rose, the Lily, the Dove)
Wenn ich in deine Augen seh' (When in your eyes I find my own)
Ich will meine Seele tauchen (I'll take my soul and give it)
Im Rhein, im heiligen Strome (The Rhine)
Ich grolle nicht (What care I now)
Und wüssten's die Blumen (If only the little flowers)
Das ist ein Flöten und Geigen (You hear the trumpets)
Hör ich das liedchen klingen (Sometimes I catch the echoes)
Ein Jüngling liebt' ein Mädchen (A boy and girl were courting)
Am leuchtenden Sommermorgen (On a golden Summer morning)
Ich hab' im Traum geweinet (I wept as I lay dreaming)
Allnächtlich im Traume (In dreams I see you)
Aus alten Märchen (Fairyland)
Die alten, bösen Lieder (I've laid my heart to sleep)

II

SEVEN SONNETS OF MICHELANGELO   *Benjamin Britten*

SONNET XVI   Just as there is a high, a low, and a middle style in pen and ink, and as within the marble are images rich and poor, according as our fancy knows how to draw them forth : ¶ so within your heart, dear love, there are perhaps, as well as pride, some humble feelings : but I draw thence only what is my desert and like to what I show outside on my face : ¶ whoever sows sighs, tears and lamentations (Heaven's moisture on earth, simple and pure, adapts itself differently to different seeds) reaps and gathers grief and sadness : ¶ whoever looks on high beauty with so great a grief reaps doubtful hopes and sure and bitter pain.

SONNET XXXI   Why must I go on venting my ardent desire in tears and melancholy words, if Heaven that dresses the soul in grief, never, soon or late, allows relief ? ¶ Why should my weary heart long for death since all must die ?   So to these eyes my last hours will be less painful, all my grief being greater than any joy.   ¶ If, therefore, I cannot avoid these blows, nay, even seek them, since it is my fate, who is the one that stands always between joy and grief ?   ¶ If to be happy I must be conquered and held captive, no wonder then that I, unarmed and alone, remain the prisoner of a Cavalier in arms.

P.T.O.

SONNET XXX   With your lovely eyes I see a sweet light that yet with my blind ones I cannot see ; with your feet I carry a weight on my back which with my lame ones I cannot ; with your wings I, wingless, fly ; with your spirit I move forever heavenward ; at your wish I blush or turn pale, cold in the sunshine, or hot in the coldest midwinter. ¶ My will is in your will alone, my thoughts are born in your heart, my words are on your breath. ¶ Alone, I am like the moon in the sky which our eyes cannot see save that part which the sun illumines.

SONNET LV   Thou know'st, beloved, that I know thou know'st that I am come nearer to enjoy thee more ; and thou know'st that I know thou know'st that I am still the same.   Why, then, do I hesitate to greet thee ?   ¶ If the hope thou givest me is true, if true the strong desire that is granted me, the wall between us crumbles, for secret griefs have double force. ¶ If I love in thee, beloved, only what you lovest most, do not be angry ; for so one spirit is enamoured of another. ¶ That which in thy lovely face I yearn for and seek to grasp, is but ill understood by human kind, and he that would see it, first must die.

SONNET XXXVIII   Give back to my eyes, you fountains and rivers, the waves of those strong currents that are not yours, which make you swell and grow with greater power than is your natural way. ¶ And thou, heavy air, that dims the heavenly light to my sad eyes, so full of my sighs art thou, give them back to my weary heart and lighten thy dark face to my eye's keen sight.   ¶ Earth, give me back my footsteps that the grass may sprout again where it was trod ; and Echo, yet deaf to my laments, give back thine sound ; and you blest pupils give back to my eyes their glances. ¶ That I another time may love another beauty, since with me you are not satisfied.

SONNET XXXII   If love be chaste and pity heavenly, and if fortune equal between two lovers ; if a bitter fate is shared by both, and if one spirit, one will rules two hearts ; ¶ if in two bodies one soul is made eternal, raising both to heaven on the same wings ; if at one stroke and with a gilded arrow love burns and pierces two hearts to the core :   ¶ if in loving one another, forgetting one's self, with one pleasure and one delight there is such reward that both wills strive for the same end ;   ¶ if thousands and thousands do not make one hundredth part to such a bond of love, to such constancy, can, then, mere anger break and dissolve it ?

SONNET XXIV   Noble soul, in whose chaste and dear limbs are reflected all that nature and heaven can achieve with us, the paragon of their works.   ¶ Graceful soul, within whom one hopes and believes Love, Pity and Mercy are dwelling, as they appear in your face ; things so rare and never found in beauty so truly. ¶ Love takes me captive, and Beauty binds me ; Pity and Mercy with sweet glances fill my heart with a strong hope.   ¶ What law or earthly government, what cruelty now or to come, could forbid Death to spare such a lovely face ?

English Translation by E. M. and P. P.

STEINWAY PIANOFORTE

THURSDAY, OCTOBER 22ND, 1942   PRICE ONE PENNY

160 *Amityville.* The Mayers' Visitors' Book. This page includes the last entry for Britten and Pears, made on 16 March 1942, in which Britten refers back to the first entry from 1939. (*See No.115.*)

161 *London.* The programme of a wartime National Gallery Concert on 22 October 1942, the autumn of the year in which Britten and Pears returned to the UK. The English translation of the Sonnets was done by Mrs Mayer (E.M.) and Pears (P.P.).

162-9 Some of the London houses in which Britten lived. *Photos* Jack Phipps.

162 559 Finchley Road, N.W.3 (1935-7).
163 45A St John's Wood High Street, N.W.8 (1943-6).
164 22 Melbury Road, W.14 (1948-53).
165 5 Chester Gate, N.W.1 (1953-8).
166 59 Marlborough Place, N.W.8 (1958-65).
167 99 Offord Road, N.1 (1965-70).
168 Halliford Street – The Studio.
169 8 Halliford Street, N.1 (1970-76).

162 · 165 · 167
163 · 166 · 168
164 · 169

170 Britten in the 1940s.
171 Britten. An unidentified photograph. It might possibly belong to 1946 when Britten visited Holland and Belgium on tour with Pears, or to 1947, when the EOG made a European tour. (*See also No.266.*)
172 *London, August 1945*. A double portrait of Britten and Pears by Cecil Beaton.
173 *August 1945*. Two portraits of Britten by Cecil Beaton.

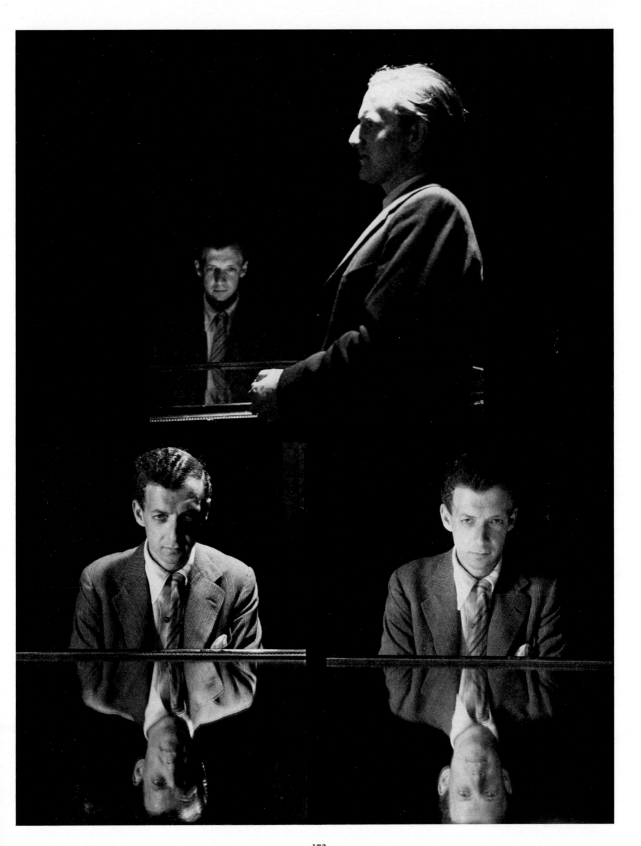

174 *London, 29 March 1944.* Concert programme at Wigmore Hall. The McPhee item is of particular interest. It was through Colin McPhee (*see No.125*) that Britten first became acquainted with Balinese music. Britten had already performed these transcriptions with McPhee during his USA years and indeed made a gramophone recording with McPhee of the complete set of pieces. His involvement with oriental music certainly had its origins at this time, though it was not to flower substantially until very much later in works like *The Prince of the Pagodas*, Op.57 (1956), *Curlew River*, Op.71 (1964), and *Death in Venice*, Op.88 (1973). It was not until 1956 that he actually visited Bali itself. (*See Nos. 296-8.*)

175 *London, c.1953.* Erwin Stein (1885-1958), the distinguished Austrian-born musician – pupil of Schoenberg – and writer who worked at Boosey & Hawkes and was Britten's close friend and adviser. *The Rape of Lucretia*, Op.37, was dedicated to him. His daughter, Marion (now Mrs Jeremy Thorpe), was to become an intimate friend of Britten and Pears and a prominent figure at Aldeburgh. (*See Nos. 261, 278 and 313.*)

176 Two pages from Balinese Ceremonial Music, transcribed by Colin McPhee and published by G. Schirmer Inc., New York, in 1940.

BALINESE CEREMONIAL
MUSIC

Transcribed for
Two Pianos,
Four-Hands

by

Colin McPhee

1. *PEMOENGKAH*
2. *GAMBANGAN*
3. *TABOEH TELOE*

NEW YORK

For Margaret Mead

Balinese Ceremonial Music

3

Transcribed for two pianos, four hands, by
Colin McPhee

1. Pemoengkah

Animato ♩=72

Piano I

Animato ♩=72

Piano II

(Soft ped.)

Lento (♩=72)   Tempo primo (♩=72)

I   rall.   *pp*

Lento (♩=72)   Tempo primo (♩=72)

II   rall.   *mp*

38797 c

WORLD
RIGHTS
CONTROLLED
by
G. SCHIRMER
Inc.

177 *London, c.1945*. Britten, back stage. The location has to be guessed, but it was probably Sadler's Wells Theatre at the time of the first production of *Peter Grimes*. *Photo* Edward Mandinian.
178 *Snape, Suffolk, c.1945*. Britten with his nephew Sebastian Welford. *Photo* Enid Slater.
179 *The Old Mill, Snape, c.1945*. Britten and Pears. *Photo* Enid Slater.

180 Kenneth Green's costume design for Peter Pears as Peter Grimes (37×25cm). (*See also Nos.231 and 235*.)
181 *Snape, 1944-5*. Britten outside the Old Mill at the time he was completing *Peter Grimes*.

SADLER'S WELLS

ROSEBERY AVENUE. E.C.1   BOX OFFICE : TER. 1672
LICENSEE : TYRONE GUTHRIE   MANAGER : GERALD SEYMOUR

THE GOVERNORS OF SADLER'S WELLS
IN ASSOCIATION WITH C.E.M.A.
PRESENT

SADLER'S WELLS OPERA

MADAM BUTTERFLY   LA BOHEME
THE BARTERED BRIDE   COSI FAN TUTTE
RIGOLETTO

AND FIRST PRODUCTION OF

PETER GRIMES

By BENJAMIN BRITTEN

ADMINISTRATORS OF THE OLD VIC AND SADLER'S WELLS COMPANIES
TYRONE GUTHRIE

THURSDAY EVE., JUNE 7TH   SATURDAY EVE., JUNE 9TH

PETER GRIMES

An Opera by BENJAMIN BRITTEN
Libretto by MONTAGU SLATER, based on the poem of George Crabbe
Conductor—REGINALD GOODALL

Peter Grimes (a Fisherman)	PETER PEARS
Ellen Orford (the Borough Schoolmistress)	JOAN CROSS
Auntie (Landlady of "The Boar")	EDITH COATES
Her " Nieces "	BLANCHE TURNER, MINNIA BOWER
Balstrode (a retired Sea-Captain)	RODERICK JONES
Mrs. Sedley (a Widow)	VALETTA IACOPI
Swallow (Lawyer and Magistrate)	OWEN BRANNIGAN
Ned Keene (Apothecary)	EDMUND DONLEVY
Bob Boles (a Methodist Fisherman)	MORGAN JONES
The Rector	TOM CULBERT
Hobson (The Village Carrier)	FRANK VAUGHAN
Doctor Thorp	SASA MACHOV
A Boy (Grimes' new apprentice)	LEONARD THOMPSON

The People of the Borough : Maude Boughton, Muriel Burnett, Peggy Butler, Rose Carlton, Myfanwy Edwards, Pauline Guy, Hilda Hanson, Netta Leggat, Jean Mountford, Winifred Newnham, Olwen Price, Keturah Sorrell, Molly Wilkinson ; Howard Allport, Gilbert Bailey, William Benn, William Booth, Albert Digney, George Gorst, Eldon Guller, Leonard Hanks, John Havard, Leonard Hodgkinson, Ivor Ingham, Cecil Lloyd, Haydn Meredith, Charles Miller, Arthur Perrow, Erin Tosi, Herbert Tree, Rhys Williams, Vaughan Williams ; Margaret Aspin, Romayne Austin, Barbara Fewster, Fiona Moore.

The action of the opera takes place in THE BOROUGH, a small East Coast Fishing-town, early in the nineteenth century

ACT I —Prologue — — — — — A Court Room in the Moot Hall
    Scene I — — — — — The High Street. A few days later
    Scene 2 — — — Inside "The Boar." The same evening

ACT II —Scene I — — — — The High Street. Some weeks later
    Scene 2 — — — — — — Peter Grimes' hut

ACT III—Scene I — — — — The High Street. Three days later
    Scene 2 — — — The same. Early the following morning

(NOTE.—The Management would be grateful if applause were reserved until after the final scene of each act, as the musical action is continuous.

Produced by ERIC CROZIER
Scenery and Costumes by KENNETH GREEN

Scenery made in Sadler's Wells Workshops and painted by Henry Bird. Costumes made in the Sadler's Wells Workrooms under the direction of Maria Garde ; and by H. Sparrow.
Properties by Harry Adams (Old Vic Workshops)   Joan Cross's Wig by Gustave
Wigs by " Bert "

THE STORY OF THE OPERA

In the life of his Suffolk fishing-town Peter Grimes fits uneasily. He lives alone, visionary, ambitious, impetuous, poaching and fishing without caution or care for consequences, and with only one friend in the town—the widowed schoolmistress, Ellen Orford. He is determined to make enough money to ask her to marry him, though too proud to ask her till he has lived down his unpopularity and remedied his poverty.

He fishes with the aid of an apprentice, bought, according to the custom of the time, from the workhouse. In the Prologue he is chief witness in an inquest on his first apprentice and the verdict is accidental death. In Act I he is boycotted but obtains a second apprentice, whom Ellen goes to fetch for him and promises to care for. In Act II she discovers he has been using the boy cruelly. Led by the Rector, the men of the Borough go to investigate his hut. Frightened, Peter takes the boy down the scar of a recent landslide under which he moors his boat, and the boy falls down the cliff. When it is discovered that the boy is dead a hue-and-cry from the Borough sets out to find Peter, who commits suicide by scuttling his boat just out of sight of the town. This is in the small hours of the morning. The Borough wakes up and goes on with its life as usual.

Musical Director	LAWRANCE COLLINGWOOD
General Manager	BRUCE WORSLEY
Stage Director	ERIC BASS
Stage Manager	JOHN GREENWOOD
Chorus Master	ALAN MELVILLE
Secretary	SHEILA FERGUSSON
General Manager (for Old Vic and Sadler's Wells)	GEORGE CHAMBERLAIN

SMOKING IS NOT PERMITTED

In accordance with the requirements of the Lord Chamberlain :
1.—The public may leave at the end of the performance by all exit doors and such doors must at that time be open.
2.—All gangways, passages and staircases must be kept entirely free from chairs or any other obstruction.
3.—Persons shall not in any circumstances be permitted to stand or sit in any of the gangways intersecting the seating, or to sit in any of the other gangways. If standing be permitted in the gangways at the sides and rear of the seating, it shall be strictly limited to the number indicated in the notices exhibited in those positions.
4.—The safety curtain must be lowered and raised in the presence of each audience.

182 *London, 7 June 1945.* The programme for the first night of
Peter Grimes.
183 Joan Cross examines a model of herself as Ellen Orford in the
original production of *Peter Grimes. Photo* Angus McBean.

184 *London, 1945. Peter Grimes* in production. Britten at the piano.
(The score is open at the climax (Fig. 42) of the manhunt in Act III.)
Left to right: Kenneth Green (*see Nos.231 and 235*), Eric Crozier
(*b.* 1914), the producer, and Reginald Goodall (*b.* 1900), who conducted the first performance.

185 *London, June 1945*. The Hut Scene (Act II, Scene 2): Grimes (Peter Pears) and his apprentice (Leonard Thompson). *Photo* Angus McBean.

186 *London, June 1945*. Peter Pears as Grimes. *Photo* Angus McBean.
187 *London, June 1945*. Act II, Scene 1: Ellen confronts Grimes and his apprentice. *Photo* Angus McBean.

188 *Glyndebourne, Summer 1946. The Rape of Lucretia*, Op.37, in production. Britten and Ernest Ansermet (1883-1969), who conducted the first performance, talk in the garden.

189 *Glyndebourne*. Britten and Ansermet rehearse *Lucretia* in the Organ Room.

190 An announcement from Glyndebourne Opera in 1946: 'It is hoped and intended that one or two new English works will be produced every year by the new company in collaboration with Glyndebourne.' The collaboration continued in 1947, but even by then its nature was radically changing. Though the long-term ambition was not fulfilled in the context of Glyndebourne, it was out of the performance of *Lucretia* that the English Opera Group emerged which then presented *Albert Herring* at Glyndebourne in 1947. On the programme of *Herring* the English Opera Group are billed as 'visitors', whereas *Lucretia* the previous year had been a 'Glyndebourne Production'.

191 *Glyndebourne, 12 July 1946*. The programme for the first performance of *Lucretia*.

192 *Glyndebourne, 16 July 1946*. A performance of *Lucretia* with the second cast, conducted by Reginald Goodall.

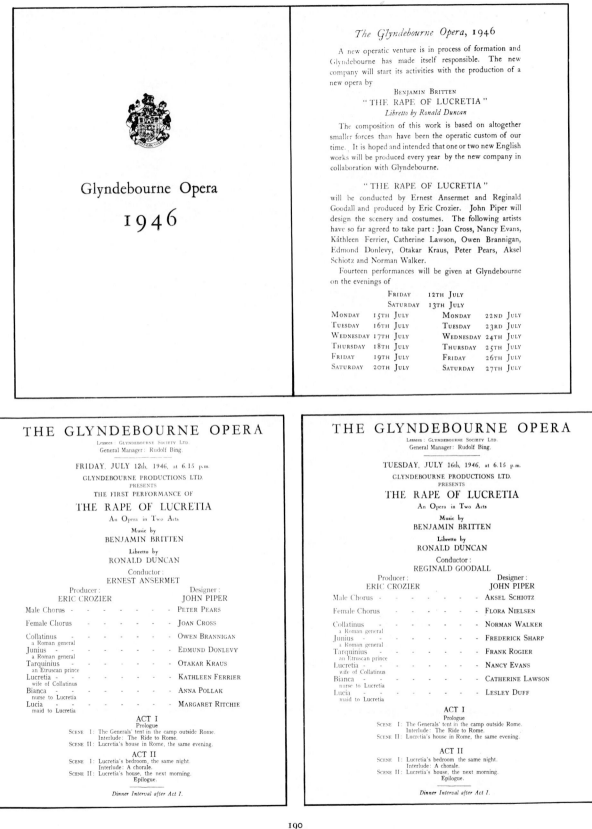

Glyndebourne Opera
1946

The Glyndebourne Opera, 1946

A new operatic venture is in process of formation and Glyndebourne has made itself responsible. The new company will start its activities with the production of a new opera by

BENJAMIN BRITTEN
"THE RAPE OF LUCRETIA"
Libretto by Ronald Duncan

The composition of this work is based on altogether smaller forces than have been the operatic custom of our time. It is hoped and intended that one or two new English works will be produced every year by the new company in collaboration with Glyndebourne.

"THE RAPE OF LUCRETIA"

will be conducted by Ernest Ansermet and Reginald Goodall and produced by Eric Crozier. John Piper will design the scenery and costumes. The following artists have so far agreed to take part: Joan Cross, Nancy Evans, Kâthleen Ferrier, Catherine Lawson, Owen Brannigan, Edmond Donlevy, Otakar Kraus, Peter Pears, Aksel Schiotz and Norman Walker.

Fourteen performances will be given at Glyndebourne on the evenings of

	FRIDAY	12TH JULY	
	SATURDAY	13TH JULY	
MONDAY	15TH JULY	MONDAY	22ND JULY
TUESDAY	16TH JULY	TUESDAY	23RD JULY
WEDNESDAY	17TH JULY	WEDNESDAY	24TH JULY
THURSDAY	18TH JULY	THURSDAY	25TH JULY
FRIDAY	19TH JULY	FRIDAY	26TH JULY
SATURDAY	20TH JULY	SATURDAY	27TH JULY

THE GLYNDEBOURNE OPERA

Lessees : GLYNDEBOURNE SOCIETY LTD.
General Manager: Rudolf Bing.

FRIDAY, JULY 12th, 1946, at 6.15 p.m.

GLYNDEBOURNE PRODUCTIONS LTD.
PRESENTS
THE FIRST PERFORMANCE OF
THE RAPE OF LUCRETIA
An Opera in Two Acts

Music by
BENJAMIN BRITTEN

Libretto by
RONALD DUNCAN

Conductor :
ERNEST ANSERMET

Producer : ERIC CROZIER   Designer : JOHN PIPER

Male Chorus	PETER PEARS
Female Chorus	JOAN CROSS
Collatinus, a Roman general	OWEN BRANNIGAN
Junius, a Roman general	EDMUND DONLEVY
Tarquinius, an Etruscan prince	OTAKAR KRAUS
Lucretia, wife of Collatinus	KATHLEEN FERRIER
Bianca, nurse to Lucretia	ANNA POLLAK
Lucia, maid to Lucretia	MARGARET RITCHIE

ACT I
Prologue
SCENE I: The Generals' tent in the camp outside Rome.
Interlude: The Ride to Rome.
SCENE II: Lucretia's house in Rome, the same evening.

ACT II
SCENE I: Lucretia's bedroom, the same night.
Interlude: A chorale.
SCENE II: Lucretia's house, the next morning.
Epilogue.

Dinner Interval after Act I.

THE GLYNDEBOURNE OPERA

Lessees : GLYNDEBOURNE SOCIETY LTD.
General Manager: Rudolf Bing.

TUESDAY, JULY 16th, 1946, at 6.15 p.m.

GLYNDEBOURNE PRODUCTIONS LTD.
PRESENTS
THE RAPE OF LUCRETIA
An Opera in Two Acts

Music by
BENJAMIN BRITTEN

Libretto by
RONALD DUNCAN

Conductor :
REGINALD GOODALL

Producer : ERIC CROZIER   Designer : JOHN PIPER

Male Chorus	AKSEL SCHIOTZ
Female Chorus	FLORA NIELSEN
Collatinus, a Roman general	NORMAN WALKER
Junius, a Roman general	FREDERICK SHARP
Tarquinius, an Etruscan prince	FRANK ROGIER
Lucretia, wife of Collatinus	NANCY EVANS
Bianca, nurse to Lucretia	CATHERINE LAWSON
Lucia, maid to Lucretia	LESLEY DUFF

ACT I
Prologue
SCENE I: The Generals' tent in the camp outside Rome.
Interlude: The Ride to Rome.
SCENE II: Lucretia's house in Rome, the same evening.

ACT II
SCENE I: Lucretia's bedroom the same night.
Interlude: A chorale.
SCENE II: Lucretia's house, the next morning.
Epilogue.

Dinner Interval after Act I.

193 *Glyndebourne, 1946.* Britten and Pears in the Organ Room.
194 *Glyndebourne, 1946.* Pears in the Organ Room.
195 *Glyndebourne, 1946.* A discussion in the theatre during rehearsals of *Lucretia* between Reginald Goodall, Britten and Rudolf Bing, who was then Glyndebourne's Director and General Manager.
196 *Glyndebourne, 1946.* Joan Cross (the Female Chorus in *Lucretia*) knits as she studies.

197 *Glyndebourne, 1946*. A rehearsal of *Lucretia* in the Organ Room, Ansermet conducting, Britten at the piano and Ronald Duncan (the librettist) turning the pages. It is the second cast that is being rehearsed, with Nancy Evans (centre) as Lucretia, and Aksel Schiotz (left) and Flora Nielsen (right) as the Male and Female Chorus. *Photo* Erich Auerbach.

198 *Glyndebourne, 1946*. Ronald Duncan (*b.* 1914), the librettist of *Lucretia*, and Britten.

199 *Glyndebourne, 1946. Lucretia.* A discussion in the Walled Garden. Left to right: Otakar Kraus, Britten, Kathleen Ferrier (1912-1953) Eric Crozier (the producer), Aksel Schiøtz, Ansermet, Nancy Evans, and Rudolf Bing.

200 *Glyndebourne, 1946.* At a performance of *Lucretia*, Ronald Duncan talks to Britten's sisters, Beth (left) and Barbara (right), who stand on either side of Mrs Ronald Duncan (Rose Marie).

201 *Glyndebourne, 1946.* Ansermet and Britten in the shrouded theatre.

202 *Glyndebourne, 1946.* The final curtain call of the first post-war season. On centre stage after a performance of *Lucretia* are (left to right) Britten, Duncan, Ansermet, John Christie, John Piper (the designer, half hidden) and Crozier.

203 *Glyndebourne, 1946.* The first production of *Lucretia*. Left to right: Margaret Ritchie (Lucia), Ferrier (Lucretia) and Anna Pollak (Bianca). *Photo* Angus McBean.

204 *Glyndebourne, 1946.* Pears and Joan Cross, the first Male and Female Chorus. *Photo* Angus McBean.

205 *Tanglewood, Mass., USA, 1946.* Britten at the Tanglewood production of *Peter Grimes*, the USA première of the opera, which was conducted by Leonard Bernstein. *Photo* Ruth Orkin, New York.
206 *Tanglewood, 1946.* Britten with Aaron Copland (*b.* 1900, centre) and Oliver Smith (the scene designer and painter). *Photo* Ruth Orkin, New York.
207 *Tanglewood, 1946.* Britten and Koussevitzky at the performance of *Grimes*. The work is inscribed: 'For the Koussevitzky Music

Foundation, dedicated to the memory of Natalie Koussevitzky.' *Photo* Ruth Orkin, New York.
208 *Tanglewood, 1946.* Britten and W.H. Auden at the performance of *Grimes. Photo* Ruth Orkin, New York.
209 *Tanglewood, 1946.* Curtain call at the end of *Grimes*. Left to right: Britten, Eric Crozier (producer) and Bernstein. *Photo* Ruth Orkin, New York.

448. PRIEST: (contd.)	Forward through the silent doubt of the desert.
	And here let me warn you: if in the forest
	You hear any voices call from the trees,
	Pay no attention, Roland, pay no attention –
449. MUSIC & GRAMS:	No. 12 *World?* (long bird-screech and into forest music; hold behind)
450. PARROT: *Vermin?*	Pretty Polly! Pretty Polly!
	Who's this coming now?
451. RAVEN:	Caw-caw! Caw-caw!
	Who's a-walkin' in my forest?
452. PARROT:	Pretty Polly! The leaves have fallen.
453. RAVEN:	Caw-caw! He's walking late.
454. PARROT:	Pretty Polly! He's looking pale.
455. RAVEN:	Caw-caw! His bones will be paler.
456. PARROT:	Pretty Polly! Here he comes.
457. RAVEN:	Caw-caw! Greet him!
458. PARROT:	Where are you going, Roland, so fast?
459. RAVEN:	Roland, running away from your past?
460. BOTH:	You can't do that! You can't do that!
461. PARROT:	Still on the road? Still on the Quest?
462. RAVEN:	None achieve it but the best.
463. BOTH:	You're not the sort. You're not the sort.
464. PARROT:	Why not stop, my dear young man?
465. RAVEN:	Let heroes die as heroes can.
466. BOTH:	You must live! You must live!
467. MUSIC:	(up forest music, then behind)
468. PARROT:	Pretty Polly! He's passed us by.
469. RAVEN:	Caw-caw! The devil take him.
470. PARROT:	Pretty Polly! The devil will.
471. MUSIC:	(up forest music, into desert music and behind)

210-11 *The Dark Tower.* A BBC radio play (21 January 1946) by Louis MacNeice (1907-1963). We show a page from the script and, by the side of it, the matching page from Britten's MS score. The juxtaposition clearly indicates the detail of the composer's response to the poet's text. Note the prophetic string glissandi in No.XII (in 1946!). (Cf. also *A Midsummer Night's Dream*, Act I prelude.)

VOICE
Sul C
Sul G
Sul A
VOICE
Sul C
Sul G
Sul A
Sul D
* All trills for Vl.1 & 2 in this number should be semitone trills
12

THE ✕◯✕◯✕◯✕◯✕◯✕◯✕◯✕◯✕◯✕

English Opera Group

✕◯✕◯✕◯✕◯✕◯✕◯✕◯✕◯✕◯✕

CHAIRMAN :
Rt. Hon. Oliver Lyttelton, D.S.O., M.C., M.P.

DIRECTORS :
Sir Kenneth Clark, K.C.B.
Mr. Tyrone Guthrie
Mr. Ralph Hawkes
Hon. Mervyn Horder
Mr. Denis Rickett
Hon. James F. A. Smith, O.B.E.
Mr. Erwin Stein

ARTISTIC DIRECTORS :
Mr. Benjamin Britten
Mr. Eric Crozier
Mr. John Piper

We believe the time has come when England, which has never had a tradition of native opera, but has always depended on a repertory of foreign works, can create its own operas. Opera is as much a vital means of artistic expression as orchestral music, drama, and painting. The lack of it has meant a certain impoverishment of English artistic life.

We believe the best way to achieve the beginnings of a repertory of English operas is through the creation of a form of opera requiring small resources of singers and players, but suitable for performance in large or small opera houses or theatres.

A first essay in this direction was the writing and staging of Britten's *The Rape of Lucretia* in 1946. *Lucretia* was an experiment towards finding a flexible and sensitive operatic form built on the collaboration of small numbers of singers, musicians and other artists. *Lucretia* was given 80 performances in 1946 — more performances than any other British opera has had in its first season, with two exceptions, since the beginning of the century.

The success of this experiment has encouraged the three persons chiefly involved — Benjamin Britten, the composer; Eric Crozier, the producer; and John Piper, the designer — to continue their work as a group by establishing, under their artistic direction, a new opera company to be known as THE ENGLISH OPERA GROUP, incorporated on a non-profit-making basis. This Group will give annual seasons of contemporary opera in English and suitable classical works including those of Purcell.

It is part of the Group's purpose to encourage young composers to write for the operatic stage, also to encourage poets and playwrights to tackle the problem of writing libretti in collaboration with composers.

2

Benjamin Britten is now writing his third opera — *Albert Herring*, a comedy about life in a Suffolk village. It is scored for 12 singers and 12 players. Its first performance, and a revival of *The Rape of Lucretia*, is planned for the Group's first season this year, which will open at Glyndebourne on June 20th. The Group hope to give a short season at the Royal Opera House, Covent Garden in early October. There will be a provincial tour, and visits to Continental festivals are under discussion.

The Group are assured of the support of many leading singers and players, and the cast for this year's season will include Joan Cross, Peter Pears, Margaret Ritchie, Nancy Evans, Otakar Kraus and Flora Nielsen. The small orchestra of leading chamber music players will include Joy Boughton, John Francis and Stephen Waters. The producers of the two operas will be Carl Ebert and Eric Crozier. The sets will be by John Piper and the conductors will be Benjamin Britten and Reginald Goodall.

The Arts Council has already generously promised financial assistance, which cannot however be expected to cover the Group's initial requirements. To enable the Group to begin work, a total sum of £12,000 is urgently needed as working capital. Of this, the sum of £2,000 has already been generously given by a private subscriber.

3

The British Council will sponsor any Continental tour undertaken by the Group, but owing to other commitments is unable to give financial assistance this year.

◯✕◯✕◯✕◯✕◯✕◯✕◯✕◯✕◯✕◯✕◯

All communications should be addressed to:

THE GENERAL MANAGER
ENGLISH OPERA GROUP

Temporary Address :
295, REGENT STREET, LONDON, W.1.

◯✕◯✕◯✕◯✕◯✕◯✕◯✕◯✕◯✕◯✕◯

212 *London, 1947.* The announcement of the formation of the English Opera Group, which now sought funds and supporters.

213 *Glyndebourne, Summer 1947.* In the restaurant. Left to right: Eric Crozier (librettist), A. Huntley Garden (Glyndebourne's stage director), Britten and John Piper. The occasion was probably the first production of *Albert Herring*.

214 *Glyndebourne, 12 July 1947.* The programme for a performance of *Albert Herring*, Op.39 (The first performance had been given on 20 June.) Note the details of the English Opera Group, which was undertaking its first season.

GLYNDEBOURNE

Lesses: GLYNDEBOURNE SOCIETY LTD.

Artistic Director: Carl Ebert   Director and General Manager: Rudolf Bing

SATURDAY, JULY 12th, 1947

THE ENGLISH OPERA GROUP LTD.

WHO COME AS VISITORS TO GLYNDEBOURNE, PRESENT

in association with THE ARTS COUNCIL OF GREAT BRITAIN

ALBERT HERRING

A Comic Opera in Three Acts

Music by	Libretto by	Designed by
BENJAMIN BRITTEN	ERIC CROZIER	JOHN PIPER

Conductor:	Producer:
BENJAMIN BRITTEN	FREDERICK ASHTON

Lady Billows an elderly autocrat	- - -	JOAN CROSS
Florence her housekeeper		GLADYS PARR
Miss Wordsworth Head Teacher at the School		MARGARET RITCHIE
Mr. Gedge the Vicar	- - -	WILLIAM PARSONS
Mr. Upfold the Mayor	- - -	ROY ASHTON
Superintendent Budd	- - -	NORMAN LUMSDEN
Sid butcher's shophand	- - -	FREDERICK SHARP
Albert Herring from the greengrocer's	-	PETER PEARS
Nancy from the bakery	-	NANCY EVANS
Mrs. Herring Albert's mother	-	BETSY DE LA PORTE
Emmie Cis } tiresome village children Harry	- - -	LESLEY DUFF ANNE SHARP DAVID SPENSER

The scene is Loxford, a small market town in East Suffolk, in the year 1900

ACT ONE (April)—SCENE I: The morning room of Lady Billows' house.
Interlude: The Village Children.
SCENE II: Mrs. Herring's greengrocer's shop.

ACT TWO (May Day)—SCENE I: A marquee in the Rectory garden.
Interlude: May Day Feast and Nocturne.
SCENE II: The greengrocer's shop.

ACT THREE (May the Second)—The greengrocer's shop.

Dinner Interval after Act One.

THE ENGLISH OPERA GROUP

First Season 1947

	Artistic Directors:	
BENJAMIN BRITTEN	ERIC CROZIER	JOHN PIPER

Conductors:	Assistant Conductor:
BENJAMIN BRITTEN, REGINALD GOODALL	IVAN CLAYTON

Designer:	Producers:
JOHN PIPER	FREDERICK ASHTON, ERIC CROZIER

Musical Assistants:
ALAN MELVILLE   NORMAN FRANKLIN   HENRY BOYS   DOROTHY ERHART

Stage Director:	Stage Manager:
ERIC CROALL	ALICE LIDDERDALE

THE ENGLISH OPERA GROUP CHAMBER ORCHESTRA

1st Violin—Jack Kessler.	*Flute*—John Francis.
2nd Violin—David Wolfsthal.	*Oboe*—John Wolfe.
Viola—Bernard Davis.	*Clarinet*—Stephen Waters.
Violoncello—George Roth.	*Bassoon*—Edward Wilson.
Double Bass—Robert Meyer.	*Horn*—David Burditt.
Harp—Enid Simon.	*Percussion*—Herbert Wilson.

Frederick Ashton and Reginald Goodall appear by permission of the Administrator of the Covent Garden Trust.

Scenery built by the AMBASSADORS SCENIC STUDIOS and painted under the supervision of Charles Bravery.

Women's costumes, hats and flowers executed by the JOHN LEWIS PARTNERSHIP.

Men's costumes by C. I. SAMUELS and EDWARD H. SPARROW.

Wigs by GUSTAVE.

Shoes by ANELLO AND DAVIDE.

Properties made by E. D. WILSON and by WILLSON AND HOPPER.

THE GLYNDEBOURNE FESTIVAL PERFORMANCE

OF

ORFEO

THE DECCA RECORD CO. LTD. have pleasure in announcing that they are making a "ffrr" recording of Orfeo, with Kathleen Ferrier, Ann Ayars, Zoë Vlachopoulos, the Southern Philharmonic Orchestra conducted by Fritz Stiedry, and the Glyndebourne Festival Chorus in the Glyndebourne production by Carl Ebert.

215 *Glyndebourne, 1947.* A discussion of *Herring* in the Walled Garden. Left to right: Frederick Ashton, Crozier, Britten and Pears.

216 *Glyndebourne, 1947.* Britten and Frederick Ashton at a rehearsal of *Albert Herring*, which Ashton produced.

217 John Piper, the painter and designer (*b.* 1903). One of Britten's oldest friends and a long-standing artistic collaborator. Piper was one of the founders of the English Opera Group. He was responsible for designing almost all Britten's major theatrical works after *Grimes* (the only exceptions were *The Beggar's Opera*, *Noye's Fludde*, the three Church Parables and the TV production of *Owen Wingrave* —as distinct from the Covent Garden production which he did design). He made a remarkably personal and sustained contribution to the production of Britten's operas, which was further strengthened by the role of his wife, Myfanwy, as librettist of *The Turn of the Screw*, *Owen Wingrave* and *Death in Venice*. (*See also Nos.262 and 265.*)

218 *Glyndebourne, 1947.* A discussion of *Herring* breaks up. Left to right: Crozier, Piper and Britten (Pears almost totally hidden behind Britten).

219 *Cambridge, May 1948*. Britten plays (and clearly, sings) his realization of *The Beggar's Opera* to Tyrone Guthrie (producer) and Tanya Moiseiwitsch (designer).
220 *Arts Theatre, Cambridge, 24 May 1948*. Guthrie and Britten during an interval at the first performance of *The Beggar's Opera* which the composer conducted.
221 *Cambridge, May 1948*. Time off from rehearsals of *The Beggar's Opera*. Eric Crozier, Nancy Evans and Peter Pears walk the Backs.
222 *Cambridge, May 1948*. *The Beggar's Opera*. Peter Pears as Macheath and Nancy Evans as Polly Peachum.

1948

THE ALDEBURGH FESTIVAL

JUNE 5th - JUNE 12th

CHAIRMAN OF EXECUTIVE COMMITTEE: THE COUNTESS OF CRANBROOK

A FIRST annual Festival of Music and Painting will be held at Aldeburgh from June 5th - June, 12th 1948, in association with The Arts Council of Great Britain and The English Opera Group.

This year it will be concentrated mainly on British music and the arts connected with the eastern part of England. It will include performances of Benjamin Britten's opera, *Albert Herring*, with Joan Cross, Peter Pears, Nancy Evans, Margaret Ritchie and other members of The English Opera Group under the direction of the composer.

In the Aldeburgh Parish Church there will be recitals by a famous string quartet and a vocal and orchestral concert including works by Purcell and Lennox Berkeley (the *Stabat Mater*). Benjamin Britten and Peter Pears will give a recital of English music from Elizabethan times to the present day. Local choirs and orchestras will combine for a concert that will include the first performance of *Saint Nicholas*, a new cantata by Benjamin Britten. There will be performances of music and drama for children.

The Festival will also present exhibitions of the work of the great East Anglian painters, including Constable and Gainsborough, and of modern paintings of Suffolk. Models of the stage settings of English and Continental productions of the local Suffolk opera, *Peter Grimes*, will also be on show.

Lectures on the great literary figures of the district and on local architecture and painting will be given by notable novelists, poets and critics of today. It is planned also to organise expeditions to places of historical interest in the neighbourhood of Aldeburgh.

Accommodation for visitors to Aldeburgh and tickets for all performances and lectures will be strictly limited.

Festival programmes, tickets and lists of available accommodation in hotels and lodgings may be obtained in early January from—

THE FESTIVAL MANAGER
THF FESTIVAL OFFICE
ALDEBURGH
SUFFOLK

223 *June 1948.* A handbill issued in connection with the First Aldeburgh Festival.

224 The title-page of the Programme Book for the First Aldeburgh Festival, 1948.

225 *1948. The First Aldeburgh Festival.* Britten and Pears outside Aldeburgh Parish Church.

226 *1949.* Outside the Jubilee Hall: the interval during an event at the Second Aldeburgh Festival. The Festival's President, Lord Harewood, in conversation. At the right front of the photograph is Eric Crozier with his back to the camera. *Photo* Ford Jenkins.

227 *Aldeburgh*. The exterior of Crag House (4 Crabbe Street), the house on the sea front where Britten and Pears lived from 1947 to 1957. *Photo* Humphrey and Vera Joel.

228 The drawing-room at Crag House with Britten's piano and harpsichord. *Photo* Humphrey and Vera Joel.

229 *Aldeburgh, c.1959*. A portrait of Britten (Clytie on his lap) by Mary Potter (oils, 76×61 cm).

230 *Aldeburgh*. Miss Hudson, Britten's housekeeper at both Crag House and The Red House: a portrait by Mary Potter (watercolour, 23×14cm).

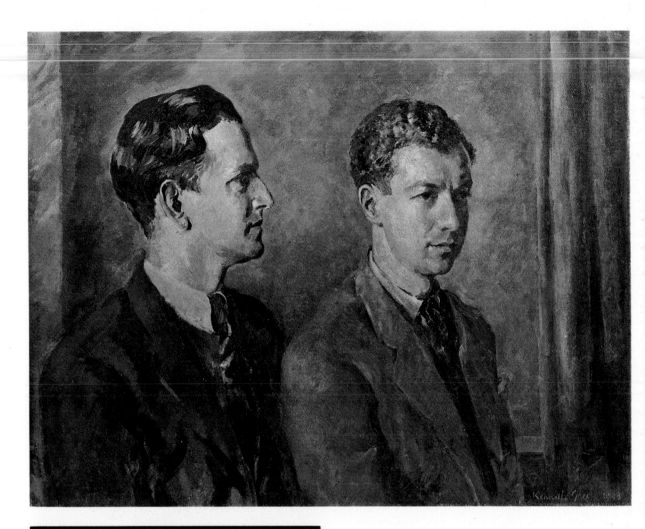

231 A double portrait of Benjamin Britten and Peter Pears by Kenneth Green (*see No.184*), signed and dated 1943 (oils, 72×98cm). Two years later the same artist was to design the costumes and sets for the 1945 production of *Peter Grimes* at Sadler's Wells. It was in 1934 that Britten briefly met Pears (*b.* 1910) for the first time, nine years before this double portrait was done. By 1943, the date of the painting, a unique creative partnership had been formed which, without exaggeration, may be claimed to be without parallel elsewhere in the history of music. It was also in 1943 that one of Britten's most

celebrated works, the *Serenade*, Op.31, for tenor, horn and strings, was composed. While in the USA he had already written for Pears the Italianate and invigorating *Seven Sonnets of Michelangelo*, Op.22 (1940), but it was perhaps the *Serenade* above all, with its miraculous interpenetration of music and English words, that embodied a moment of absolute mastery in the development of Britten's art. The work also embodied – was indeed emblematic of – the creative results of the partnership of the composer and the singer from which flowed uninterruptedly a whole succession of works until the very end of

Britten's life. It is no accident, then, that from this point onwards, what this book documents is not one life, but two. *Photo* National Portrait Gallery.

232 *1963*. Bust of Peter Pears by Georg Ehrlich.
233 *1950-52*. Bust of Britten by Georg Ehrlich.
234 *London, November 1945*. This portrait of Britten by Henry Lamb (oils, 68.5 × 56cm) was originally exhibited at the Leicester Galleries. It is now at The Red House, Aldeburgh.

235 Portrait of Britten by Kenneth Green (oils, 61 × 51cm, dated 1943).

236-7 Peter Pears, Aaron Copland and Britten. These photographs are baffling. It is possible that they belong to the USA years, but neither Copland nor Pears can precisely identify the location or the occasion. There is a further and perhaps stronger possibility that these pictures were taken in connection with Copland's *Old American Songs*, which were given their first performance by Pears and Britten at the Aldeburgh Festival on 18 June 1950 (having been commissioned by them while on their North American tour the preceding year: *see Nos.242-4*). The photographs would make sense in that context – they look very much like a composer's run-through – even though the location remains a puzzle.

238 *Aldeburgh, Jubilee Hall, 14 June 1949.* Norman Del Mar rehearses the audience in the 'Night Song' at the first performance of *Let's make an Opera.*

239 *Aldeburgh, 1949.* Britten, with the children of the original cast of *Let's make an Opera*, at the wheel of his vintage Rolls Royce.

240 *Aldeburgh, 1949. Let's make an Opera* gets under way at the Jubilee Hall, and it is probably Elizabeth Sweeting, the first Manager of the Aldeburgh Festival, who is under Sammy's bath.

241 Britten in the late 1940s. Probably Cheltenham, 1949, where the English Opera Group appeared during the Festival. (*See also No.245*, from 1949, where Britten wears the same mackintosh.) *Photo* Desmond Tripp, Bristol.

242 *New York, 23 October 1949*. Britten with Betty Randolph Bean (who accompanied Britten and Pears on their coast-to-coast recital tour of the USA), after their Town Hall recital. At that time Miss Bean was working for Boosey & Hawkes, New York. *Photo* Erich Hartmann, New York.

243 *Southampton, 1949*. Pears, Anthony Gishford and Britten.

Britten and Pears were about to embark for their tour of the USA and Canada. Anthony Gishford (1908-1975), Director of Boosey & Hawkes and Editor of *Tempo* from 1947 to 1958, became a close and valued friend of the composer. He was Chairman of the English Opera Group for many years and a Director of Faber Music from its inception. In 1963 he assembled and edited the *Tribute to Benjamin Britten on his Fiftieth Birthday* (London, 1963).

244 *New York, Town Hall, 23 October 1949*. Britten and Pears, perhaps just about to embark on an encore. *Photo* Erich Hartmann, New York.

245 *Amsterdam, 9 July 1949.* After the first performance at the Holland Festival of the *Spring Symphony*, Op.44, which had been conducted by Eduard van Beinum, the composer leaves the Concertgebouw.

246 *Amsterdam, 9 July 1949.* The first performance of the *Spring Symphony*. Left to right: Britten, Jo Vincent (soprano), van Beinum (conductor), Kathleen Ferrier (mezzo-soprano) and Pears (tenor).

𝔅𝔬𝔯𝔬𝔲𝔤𝔥 𝔬𝔣 𝔏𝔬𝔴𝔢𝔰𝔱𝔬𝔣𝔱

Statute 23 and 24 Geo. 5. C. 51.

Programme of the Ceremony

OF

PRESENTATION

OF THE

Honorary
Freedom of the Borough

TO

BENJAMIN BRITTEN, Esq.

AT

SPARROW'S NEST THEATRE, LOWESTOFT,

On Saturday, 28th July, 1951.

COUNCILLOR W. H. AMY, J.P., (Mayor).
F. B. NUNNEY, Esq., M.A., Town Clerk.

247 *1951.* The programme of the ceremony in which Britten received the Freedom of the Borough of Lowestoft, his birth-place. (For an earlier appearance at the Sparrow's Nest, *see No.15.*)
248 *London, Royal Festival Hall, 12 December 1951.* Britten, Sir Thomas Beecham and the American violinist Bronislaw Gimpel after a rehearsal, with the Royal Philharmonic Orchestra, of Britten's Violin Concerto.

249 *Birmingham, 22 January 1952.* Pears, Ferrier and Britten on a tour in aid of the English Opera Group, during which a new work was given its first performance at Nottingham on 21 January: Canticle II, *Abraham and Isaac*, Op.51 (text from the Chester Miracle Play), for alto, tenor and piano.

250 *Aldeburgh, 1950*. E.M. Forster (1879-1970), Britten and Eric Crozier at Crag House, working on the libretto of *Billy Budd*.

251 *Aldeburgh, 1950*. Britten and E.M. Forster during the writing of *Billy Budd*.

252 *London, Royal Opera House, Covent Garden, 1951*. *Billy Budd*, Op.50, which was first performed, the composer conducting, on 1 December 1951. Billy faces the drumhead court. Left to right: Geraint Evans (Mr Flint), Michael Langdon (Lieutenant Ratcliffe),

Hervey Alan (Mr Redburn), Theodor Uppman (Billy) and Peter Pears (Captain Vere). *Photo* Roger Wood.
253 *New York, 19 October 1952.* The first of Britten's operas to be televised: *Billy Budd* on NBC-TV. Left to right: Theodor Uppman (Billy), Andrew McKinley (Vere) and Leon Lishner (Claggart).
254 *London, 1951.* The American baritone Theodor Uppman, the first Billy. *Photo* Angus McBean.

THE ROYAL OPERA HOUSE, COVENT GARDEN LTD.

General Administrator - David L. Webster
Deputy General Administrator - Sir Steuart Wilson

GALA PERFORMANCE

ON THE OCCASION OF
THE CORONATION OF
HER MAJESTY
QUEEN ELIZABETH II

MONDAY, 8TH JUNE, 1953
at 8 p.m.

God Save The Queen
Arranged by SIR WILLIAM WALTON

THE COVENT GARDEN OPERA
in the first performance of

GLORIANA
OPERA IN THREE ACTS

Music by BENJAMIN BRITTEN   Libretto by WILLIAM PLOMER

Producer - BASIL COLEMAN   Scenery and Costumes by JOHN PIPER
Choreography by JOHN CRANKO   Lighting by JOHN SULLIVAN
Conductor - JOHN PRITCHARD

THE COVENT GARDEN OPERA CHORUS
Chorus Master - DOUGLAS ROBINSON

THE COVENT GARDEN ORCHESTRA
Leader - CHARLES TAYLOR

Characters in Order of Appearance

Robert Devereux, Earl of Essex	PETER PEARS
Henry Cuffe, a satellite of Essex	RONALD LEWIS
Charles Blount, Lord Mountjoy	GERAINT EVANS
Queen Elizabeth the First	JOAN CROSS
Sir Walter Raleigh, Captain of the Guard	FREDERICK DALBERG
Sir Robert Cecil, Secretary of the Council	ARNOLD MATTERS
The Recorder of Norwich	MICHAEL LANGDON
The Spirit of the Masque	WILLIAM McALPINE
Penelope (Lady Rich), sister to Essex	JENNIFER VYVYAN
Frances, Countess of Essex	MONICA SINCLAIR
A Lady-in-Waiting	ADELE LEIGH
The Master of Ceremonies	DAVID TREE
A Blind Ballad-Singer	INIA TE WIATA
A Housewife	EDITH COATES
The City Crier	RHYDDERCH DAVIES
Sir John Harington	LEONARD LAW
The French Ambassador	RONALD FIRMAGER

Solo Dancers

Concord	SVETLANA BERIOSOVA
Time	DESMOND DOYLE
Morris Dancer	JOHAAR MOSEVAAL

Citizens, Maids of Honour, Ladies and Gentlemen of the Household, Courtiers, Masquers, Old Men, Men and Boys of Essex's Following, Councillors, Country Girls, Rustics and Fishermen, Pages.

Dancers from the Sadler's Wells Ballet School
Ballet Master - HAROLD TURNER

The Children are members of the Kingsland Central School and have been trained by Mr. GEORGE HURREN

ACT I.	Scene 1:	Outside a tilting-ground
	Scene 2:	A private apartment at Nonesuch
ACT II.	Scene 1:	The Guildhall at Norwich
	Scene 2:	The garden of Essex House in the Strand
	Scene 3:	A great room in the Palace of Whitehall
ACT III.	Scene 1:	An anteroom at Nonesuch
	Scene 2:	A street in the City of London
	Scene 3:	A room in the Palace of Whitehall

God Save The Queen

---

255 The programme for the première of *Gloriana*, Op.53, at the Royal Opera House, Covent Garden, on 8 June 1953. The opera was 'dedicated by gracious permission to Her Majesty Queen Elizabeth II, in honour of whose Coronation it was composed.'

256 *Royal Opera House, Covent Garden*, 1953. A piano rehearsal of *Gloriana* in the Crush Bar. Basil Coleman, the producer, guides Jennifer Vyvyan (Penelope, Lady Rich) towards Peter Pears (back to camera, Essex). John Pritchard conducts and Britten watches from the foot of the stairs. *Photo* Roger Wood.

257 *London, 1953*. William Plomer, the poet and librettist of *Gloriana* and the three Church Parables, watched by Peter Pears. *Photo* Roger Wood.

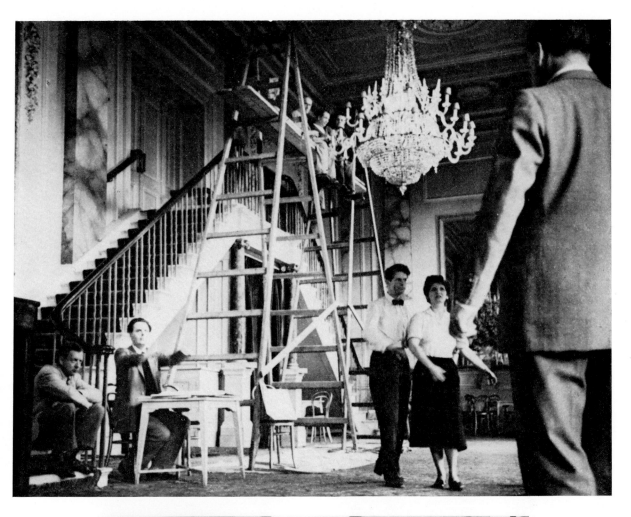

258 *The Red House, Aldeburgh, 1950s.* Britten, partnered by Mary Potter, the painter (*see Nos.229, 230, 287 and 314*), playing tennis when the house still belonged to Mary Potter and her husband, Stephen.

259 *Aldeburgh, 1950s.* Britten in formidable action on the Aldeburgh public tennis courts. He showed much cup-winning prowess when he was a boy.

260 *Copenhagen.* This remarkable photograph was discovered in 1977 in a Copenhagen junkshop by Derek Hill, the painter, who was struck by the haunting quality of the face, recognized it as Britten's and bought the photograph. The year 1947 appears as part of the information on the back of the photograph. Might it belong to, or be associated with, the production of *Peter Grimes* in Copenhagen in November 1947? It was to Derek Hill that Britten dedicated his *Hymn of St Columba* (1962). *Photo* Frederick Vogt.

261 *Venice, 1954.* At a pavement café. Left to right: Marion Harewood (now Mrs Jeremy Thorpe), Peter Diamand (then general manager of the Holland Festival), Imogen Holst (*see No.287*), Lord Harewood, Anthony Gishford, Mrs Stein, Mrs Diamand (back to camera) and Britten who may be talking to Basil Douglas. Directly behind Britten, probably Erwin Stein. *Photo* Erich Auerbach.

262 *Venice, September 1954.* A street picnic during rehearsals for the first performance of *The Turn of the Screw* at the Teatro la Fenice. Left to right: John Piper (designer), Britten, Pears (Quint), Edward Piper, Basil Douglas (the Manager of the English Opera Group), Clarissa Piper and Myfanwy Piper (the librettist). *Photo* Erich Auerbach.

263 Jennifer Vyvyan (1925-1974), the soprano, a prominent member of the English Opera Group. She created the roles of the Governess in *The Turn of the Screw*, Tytania in *A Midsummer Night's Dream* and Mrs Julian in *Owen Wingrave*. (*See also No.356*.)

264 Basil Coleman, the producer. His productions of Britten's operas include *Billy Budd* (1951), *Gloriana* (1953) and *The Turn of the Screw* (1954). He also produced *Billy Budd* for BBC-TV, which was first screened on 11 December 1966. *Photo* Maiteny, London.

265 *Venice, 14 September 1954.* The curtain call at the first night of *The Turn of the Screw*. Left to right: Joan Cross (Mrs Grose, barely visible), David Hemmings (Miles), Jennifer Vyvyan (Governess), Britten (who conducted), Myfanwy Piper and Basil Coleman (producer). *Photo* Erich Auerbach.

266 *Switzerland, 1947?*. Britten, who was not often photographed wearing spectacles. (*See also Nos.381 and 386.*) This may have been taken during the EOG European tour of *Herring* in 1947. *Photo* Hänssler, Zürich.

267 A cartoon by Sir David Low, *c.1950*. *Photo* University of Hull Art Collection.

268 Britten in 1951.

269 *Aldeburgh, c.1950*. Britten at his desk in Crag House, perhaps editing Purcell. *Photo* Roland Haupt.

270 *Aldeburgh, Crag House, c.1950*. Britten. *Photo* Roland Haupt.

271 *Graubünden, Switzerland, 1956.* Britten and butterfly. On holiday at Schloss Tarasp, the property of Prince Ludwig of Hesse, where Britten and Pears were frequent visitors. *Photo* Prince Ludwig of Hesse.

272 *Siena, 1956.* Pears and Britten. *Photo* Prince Ludwig of Hesse.

273 Britten at home. In the drawing-room of The Red House in the 1960s.

274 One of four working drawings for a cartoon of Britten by Sir David Low, *c.*1950. *Photo* National Portrait Gallery.

275 Schloss Tarasp. A woodcut by Reynolds Stone. (*See No.438.*)

274
275

276 A meeting of the Aldeburgh Music Club at Crag House in the 1950s. A rare photograph of Britten playing the viola. It was the Schubert Quintet that was being performed. Left to right: Miss Rhoda Backhouse, Miss Biddie Row, Miss Dot Row, a visitor from the USA and Britten.

277 *Aldeburgh, Suffolk, mid-1950s.* Britten and Pears playing recorders in the garden of Crag House.

278 *Aldeburgh Festival, 1957.* Music on the Meare at Thorpeness. Britten, Prince Ludwig of Hesse, Marion Harewood (now Thorpe) and Princess Margaret of Hesse. Prince Ludwig (1908-1968) and Princess Margaret, close friends of Britten and Pears, often their travelling companions, were generous patrons and benefactors of the Aldeburgh Festival (the Hesse students), a tradition continued by the Princess. As 'Ludwig Landgraf' Prince Ludwig was responsible for

among other things, the German translations of *The Turn of the Screw*, *Noye's Fludde*, the *War Requiem* (with Fischer-Dieskau) and the first two of the Church Parables. Britten inscribed his *Six Hölderlin Fragments*, Op.61 (1958), to Prince Ludwig for his fiftieth birthday. (First performance given at Schloss Wolfsgarten (*see No.396*) on 20 November 1958 by Pears and the composer.)
279 *Aldeburgh Festival, 1957 or 1958.* Imogen Holst conducts music on the Meare.

280-3 *The Red House, Aldeburgh, 1958.* Britten and Menuhin rehearse Mozart's Violin Sonata in A major, K. 402, for a Festival concert at Framlingham Church on 22 June. *Photos* Kurt Hutton.

284 *Blythburgh Church, Suffolk, 16 June 1957.* Britten rehearses (for a recital with Menuhin) and Imogen Holst turns the pages. *Photo* Ian Graham.

285 Britten's studio at Crag House, with its view of the sea. *Photo* Humphrey and Vera Joel.

286 His studio at The Red House, overlooking the garden.

287 *1954*. Portrait of Imogen Holst by Mary Potter (oils, 71 × 56cm). In 1952 Imogen Holst became Britten's music assistant, a position she retained until 1964. In 1956 she was appointed an Artistic Director of the Aldeburgh Festival, retiring in 1977. No caption could adequately contain all her gifts or represent the contribution she has made to music at Aldeburgh as scholar, writer, editor, conductor, composer and Festival planner, and above all as an intimate colleague of Britten for twelve years. Her monograph on Britten was first published in 1966 and she collaborated with him in writing *The Story of Music*, first published in 1958. She continues with many aspects of her work and her remarkable presence is not only part of Aldeburgh but of musical life throughout the country.

288 *Amsterdam, 1951.* Britten and Joan Cross at Schipol airport. The English Opera Group was to perform a double bill at the Holland Festival: Monteverdi's *Combattimento* and Purcell's *Dido*, the new realization of which Britten had recently completed with Imogen Holst. The *Dido* was Nancy Evans, Joan Cross produced and Britten conducted from the harpsichord.

289 *Amsterdam, 1951.* Sampling Bols.

290 *Venice, 1956.* Britten and Pears with Prince Ludwig and Princess Margaret of Hesse on the Grand Canal (the Rialto bridge in the background).

291 *Cannes, c.1956.* Pears and Britten, with Francis Poulenc (1899–1963).

292 *Stratford, Ont., Canada, August 1957.* Britten and Pears. The English Opera Group performed *The Turn of the Screw* at the Stratford Festival in August and September.

293 *Kyoto, Japan, February 1956.* The Tea Ceremony. Britten and Pears face the camera. Facing Britten, Prince Ludwig of Hesse. The visit to Japan, which was based on Tokyo, was part of the long trip to the Far East which Britten and Pears made in the company of Prince Ludwig and Princess Margaret of Hesse in the winter of 1955-6. The tour began in Europe in November and then progressed eastwards.

294 *India, December 1955?.* Britten and Pears at breakfast.

295 *Macau, 4 February 1956.* Britten and Pears gave a recital in the eighteenth-century theatre there.

296 *Ubud, Bali, January 1956.* Pears, Prince Ludwig, Princess Margaret and Britten in traditional Balinese costume. About this photograph Princess Margaret wrote home on 21 January: 'Our very primitive life . . . in Ubud continued to be very colourful. [Our host] made us put on Balinese dress and be photographed. I . . . wrapped in a sarong with a lace curtain over my ample bust,

beautiful gardenias in my hair (a false *black* pigtail had been added) looked too stupid for words. Ben also togged up looked like a governess at a fancy dress. Peter looked like a Rhine Maiden and Lu [Prince Ludwig] like a *Fasching* Rajah! We laughed so much we could hardly be photographed!'

297 *Bali, 1956.* 'The dancing lesson', with a Balinese *gamelan* accompanying the teacher and pupil. Britten wrote about Bali to Imogen Holst from Ubud on 17 January: '. . . the island where

musical sounds are as [much] part of the atmosphere as the palm trees, spicy smells, and the charming, beautiful people. The music is *fantastically* rich – melodically, rhythmically, texture (such *orchestration*!!) and above all *formally*. It's a remarkable culture . . . . At last I'm beginning to catch on to the technique, but it's about as complicated as Schönberg.'

298 *Bali, 1956.* Britten in Tenganan, the old village in the hills to the east of Bali.

299 *1958. Noye's Fludde.* Mr Squirrel (André Ravasio) and Mr Britten. (The costumes and masks were designed by Ceri Richards.) *Photo* Kurt Hutton.

300 *1958. Noye's Fludde.* An early percussion rehearsal. Britten demonstrates the slung mugs. *Photo* Kurt Hutton.

301 *Orford Church, Suffolk, June 1958.* Britten among the audience at the dress rehearsal of *Noye's Fludde*, Op.59, the first performance of which was given on 18 June.

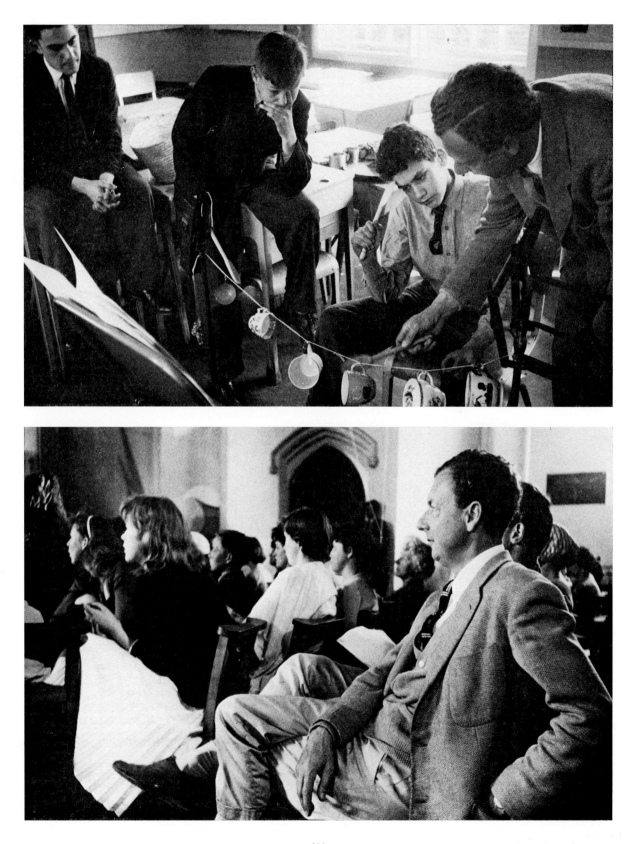

PRAISE WE GREAT MEN

EDITH SITWELL

For Benjamin Britten

Praise we the Gods of Sound—
From all the hearths and homes of men, from hives
Of honey-making lives ;
Praise with our music those
Who bring the morning light
To the hearts of men, those households of high heaven ! Praise

We the great Gods of Sound
Who stole the honey-red, the frozen fire—
Oh, beyond all delight and all desire—
From gilded hives upon Mount Parnassus
(Hives gilded by the light)—who brought to us
That fire compressed into such holy forms,
As those of the gold wanderers in heaven ! Praise

Those who can raise
Gold spirits of mankind from the rough ape-dust, and can show
The planetary system in the Atom, and great suns
Hid in a speck of dust. Praise we the just
Who have not come to judge, but come to bless
Immortal things in our poor earthly dress
And ripen lives and rule our hearts and rhythms,
Immortal hungers in the veins and heart.

Praise be to those who sing
Green hymns of the great waters to the dry
And tearless deserts in the souls of men, until
Under the fertilisation of their singing breath
Even the greyness and the dust of Death
Seem the grey pollen of the long September heat.

Oh, praise

With lion-music such as that heard in the air
When the roaring golden lion that roams the heavens
Devours the dark, and multitudes and magnitudes respond

To that lion-music . . . and on wings
Of music let us rise
Like velvet honey-flies
To praise the Gods of Sound with those bee-murmurings

The sound of violins
And the clear sound of flutes
As round as honeyed fruits
And like the water-Phoenix ever rising
For wanderers in the lonely desert-sand.

Praise we these earthly Gods,
Praise with the trumpet's purple sound—
Praise with the trumpet-flower
And with that flower the long five-petalled hand
That sweeps the strings. Praise with that angel of High God
the voice !
Oh, let us still rejoice
And praise we these great men from the first hour
Of the spirit's birth until our earthly setting

Into the night of Death.
Praise with our last breath
These earthly Gods who bring
All sounds, all faiths, delights and splendours lost
Beneath the winter's frost
Back to the hearts, the hearths and homes of men.

Fires on the hearth, fires in the skies, fires in the human heart,
Praise we Great Men !

© *Dame Edith Sitwell, 1959*

302 *London, Royal Festival Hall, 10 June 1959.* The Royal Philharmonic Society concert, the first half of which was conducted by Britten and prefaced by Edith Sitwell reading a new poem, 'Praise We Great Men', dedicated to Britten. It was this text, published for the first time in this programme, to which Britten returned in 1976. (*See No.439.*)

303 Dame Edith Sitwell (1887-1964). Britten's Canticle III, *Still falls the Rain*, Op.55, for tenor voice, horn and piano (1954), was a setting of a poem by Dame Edith, who wrote to the composer after the first performance on 28 January 1955 at the Wigmore Hall: 'I am so haunted and so alone with that wonderful music and its wonderful performance that I was incapable of writing before now. I had no sleep at all on the night of the performance. And I can think of nothing else. It was certainly one of the greatest experiences in all my life as an artist . . . . I can never begin to thank you for the glory you have given my poem . . . .' (26 April 1955. From *Edith Sitwell: Selected Letters*, ed. J. Lehmann and D. Parker, London, 1970, p.191.)

304 Purcell. 'Hark the ech'ing air!'. The first MS page of Britten's realization. The words are in Pears' hand.

Hark the echoing air!
In B♭
Allegro moderato
Voice
Piano
Hark hark the echoing air a tri— umph sings—
f (mf)
8va
tri— umph, a tri
p
umph, tri-umph sing
, a tri umph tri-umph sings

305 *Aldeburgh, 1961.* The first run-through of the Sonata in C, Op.65, for cello and piano. Britten and Mstislav Rostropovitch (the dedicatee) in the studio at The Red House, with members of the English Chamber Orchestra listening. *Photo* Erich Auerbach.
306 *Aldeburgh, 1961.* After the run-through. *Photo* Erich Auerbach.
307 *Aldeburgh, 1961.* Rostropovitch, Galina Vishnevskaya (Madame Rostropovitch), Britten and Pears in the drive of The Red House. *Photo* Erich Auerbach.
308 Vishnevskaya and Britten. *Photo* Erich Auerbach.

Borough of Aldeburgh

PRESENTATION

OF THE

Honorary
Freedom of the Borough

TO

BENJAMIN BRITTEN, Esq., C.H.

by

HIS WORSHIP THE MAYOR OF ALDEBURGH
(Mr. Councillor C. H. H. Smith, J.P.)

On Monday, 22nd October, 1962, at 7 p.m.

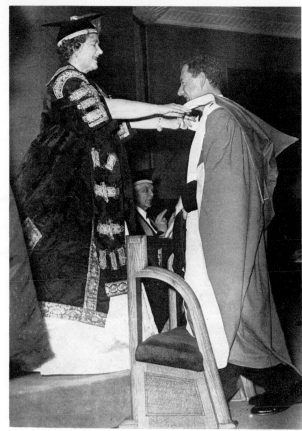

309 *Aldeburgh, 22 October 1962.* Britten receives the Honorary Freedom of the Borough of Aldeburgh from His Worship the Mayor of Aldeburgh (Mr Councillor C.H.H. Smith, JP) at the Moot Hall. *Photo* B.W. Allen, Aldeburgh.

310 The programme for the ceremony.

311 *University of London, 26 November 1964.* The Queen Mother, the Chancellor of the University, confers the honorary degree of Doctor of Music on Britten as part of the University's foundation day celebrations.

312 *St Michael's Cathedral, Coventry, 30 May 1962.* A rehearsal for the first performance of the *War Requiem*, Op.66, at the festival to celebrate the consecration of the re-built St Michael's Cathedral, Coventry. At the centre of the photograph Britten, who conducted the chamber orchestra, talks to the principal conductor, Meredith Davies. The soloists at the première were Peter Pears (standing, right), Dietrich Fischer-Dieskau (seated, on Pears' right) and Heather Harper (not in view). *Photo* Erich Auerbach.

313 *Moscow, March 1963*. Britten was in the USSR for a festival of British music organized by the British Council. This photograph shows him in Red Square with Pears, Vishnevskaya, Rostropovitch and Marion Harewood (now Thorpe). *Photo* E. I. Iavno.

314 *France, 1960s*. On holiday. Britten took this snap of Pears and their travelling companion Mary Potter, the painter. Britten's Alvis stands in the background. *Photo* BB.

315 *Aspen, Colorado, USA, July 1964*. Britten travelled to Aspen, Colorado, to receive the first Aspen Award and to deliver there his speech of thanks (*On Receiving the First Aspen Award*, published in 1964). In this photograph he sits between Alvin C. Eurich, President of the Aspen Institute, and (in hat) Robert O. Anderson, the creator of the Award. *Photo* Ferenc Berko, Aspen, Colorado.

our host took a torch and showed us Pushkin's house and museum, and outside the front door was the clock tower and its cracked clock which was there in Pushkin's time and still struck its old hours. Simple six-roomed one-floored house, while the two caretakers, a man and his round wife, held up candles to the dark pictures and framed MSS. on the walls, and the brass bedstead and the fastenings on the stove glittered. We saw the little house where Pushkin's beloved Nana lived, her ikons on the shelf by the stove, her spinning-wheel and the clasp which held the thin strips of wood which lit the little rooms in those days. There was too the house of the bailiff, simple and austere, all wood, neatly clean.

After a meal of soup and excellent cold leg of lamb, and a sort of barley with meat balls (so good), marvellous coffee and plum syrup, our host begged to hear the Pushkin songs. We moved into the lamp-lit sitting-room with an upright piano in the corner, and started on the songs (after an introduction by Slava). Galya sang her two, and I hummed the others. The last song of the set is the marvellous poem of insomnia, the ticking clock, persistent night-noises and the poet's cry for a meaning in them. Ben has started this with repeated staccato notes high-low high-low on the piano. Hardly had the little old piano begun its dry tick tock tick tock, than clear and silvery outside the window, a yard from our heads, came ding, ding, ding, not loud but clear, Pushkin's clock joining in his song. It seemed to strike far more than midnight, to go on all through the song, and afterwards we sat spell-bound. It was the most natural thing to have happened, and yet unique, astonishing, wonderful. In the morning, from our windows we could see the still silver pond beyond the field, with clumps of silver birches far away, and the great forest of enor-mously tall, enormously thin fir-trees. Not far off was the village church, to which Pushkin in his exile was commanded to report for worship every day at 1 p.m. (so we were told). It is a simple, pleasant and spacious little country-church with a bulbous dome, and is approached up a flight of steps. In front is Pushkin's tomb, a curious un-beautiful, masonic affair, which the Germans ineffectively tried to mine as they left. They also destroyed most of the church walls and roof, and blew up the great bronze bell which summoned Pushkin to worship. The church has been rebuilt and turned into a museum —pleasantly enough. We paid our respects, and set off in uncertain weather back towards Moscow. Our hosts to whom we said farewell

36

316 *Armenia, USSR, 1965.* Outside the Composers' Home for Creative Work, Dilidjan, where Britten and Pears stayed for some three weeks. Back, left to right: Asa Amintayeva (pianist), Britten, Galina and Mstislav Rostropovitch, Pears and Alexander Arutiunyan (Armenian composer); in front, Eduard Mirzoyan (Armenian composer).
317 *Armenia, August 1965.* Britten and Rostropovitch talking. An account of Britten's and Pears' vacation trip is given in Pears'

privately printed (1966) diary, *Armenian Holiday*. During his visit to Russia Britten composed *The Poet's Echo*, Op.76, settings in the orig-inal Russian, of poems by Pushkin. These he dedicated to his hosts and holiday companions, Rostropovitch and his wife, Galina, who gave the work its first complete performance in Moscow on 2 December 1965. (Two of the songs had been performed at Yerevan in August.)
318 An excerpt from Pears' diary, *Armenian Holiday: August 1965.*

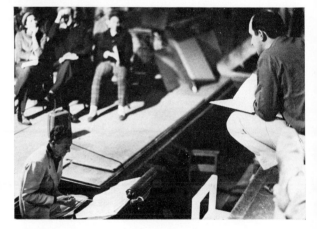

319 *Aldeburgh, Jubilee Hall, 1963.* Viola Tunnard (1916-1974) and Britten. Clearly an anxious moment during a rehearsal of *The Beggar's Opera*. Viola was a particularly valued colleague, whose distinction as an accompanist and répétiteur was legendary. *Photo* Reg Wilson.

320 *Blythburgh Church, Suffolk, 16 June 1965.* Britten and Sviatoslav Richter rehearsing Mozart's Piano Concerto in B flat, K.595, for a Festival concert.

321 *Jubilee Hall, 1963.* A rehearsal of *The Beggar's Opera*. Britten discusses a point with Colin Graham, the producer. *Photo* Reg Wilson.

322 *Blythburgh, 26 June 1964.* Rostropovitch and Britten at a rehearsal for the first English performance of the Symphony for Cello and Orchestra, Op.68, at the Aldeburgh Festival. (Its première had been given in Moscow on 12 March by the same soloist (again the dedicatee!) with the composer conducting.)

323 *Aldeburgh, 1964.* Britten and Colin Graham in the Alvis leaving The Red House. This was Britten's home from 1957 until his death in 1976.

324 *Aldeburgh, 1960s.* Britten and Clytie outside The Red House.

325 *Aldeburgh, 1972.* A snapshot of Rosamund Strode (right), Britten's meticulous music assistant, and a vital part of his working life, from 1963 until his death. She is now Secretary to the Britten Estate and Correspondent of the Britten-Pears Library. On the left is Lloyda Swatland, secretary to the General Manager of the Aldeburgh Festival. *Photo* William Servaes.

326 *November, 1958.* The wedding reception of Sylvia and Jeremy Cullum. Jeremy was Britten's secretary for seventeen years, from 1951 to 1968. He now owns the Aldeburgh Music Centre in Aldeburgh High Street. *Photo* Kurt Hutton.

327 *London, 12 February 1971.* Richard de la Mare, the first Chairman of Faber Music, from 1966 to 1971, and son of Walter de la Mare, the poet. *Photo* Mark Gerson.

328 T.S. Eliot (1888-1965), the poet and a Director of Faber & Faber from 1925 to 1965. Eliot warmly welcomed the idea of Faber's publishing Britten's music. He did not live, alas, to hear Britten's

THE RED HOUSE. ALDEBURGH. SUFFOLK.

20th March, 1964.

Dear Mr. du Sautoy,

Thank you for your kind letter of March 16th, which I got on my return from Russia.

I was delighted to know how interested you and Mr. de la Mare are in a possible music publishing branch of Faber and Faber, and I am equally pleased to know from Donald Mitchell that your colleagues on the Board are also interested in this project. I look forward very much to your coming here on April 1st and discussing the matter in some detail. I am most touched by your interest in my own music, of course, but I do feel that a lively new music publishing firm can be of the utmost value to the musical life of this country.

With best wishes.

Yours sincerely,

P. F. du Sautoy Esq.
Faber and Faber Ltd.
24 Russell Square
London W.C.1.

settings of his *Journey of the Magi* (Canticle IV) and *The Death of St Narcissus* (Canticle V) but he would surely have been touched to know that for a long period after Britten's heart operation in 1973 his poetry was among the few things Britten found himself able to read. From the authority of it he derived calm and courage. *Photo Angus McBean.*

329 Walter de la Mare (1873–1956), the poet, who was published by Faber's. Britten made settings in boyhood of de la Mare's poems. The collection of them which he published in 1969 as *Tit for Tat* is dedicated to Richard de la Mare. *Photo Mark Gerson.*

330 A letter from Britten to Peter du Sautoy, who was then Vice-Chairman of Faber & Faber, when the possibility of the firm setting up a music publishing department was first being discussed. It is characteristic that Britten's conception of this new enterprise extended beyond the boundaries of his own music. When the department evolved into a separate company in 1966 Britten became a member of the Board and remained a Director until his death.

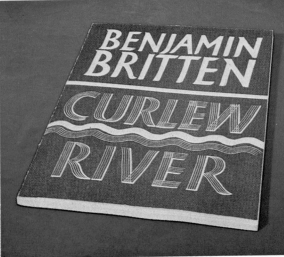

331 *Venice, February, 1968.* Palazzo Moncenigo where Britten composed the third of his Church Parables, *The Prodigal Son*, Op.81. The first Parable, *Curlew River*, Op.71, was also partly composed in Venice in the spring of 1964. Indeed, the concept of the music was actively influenced by the resonant acoustic of Venetian churches, the non-synchronizing effect of which on musical sound – above all on voices – Britten had very much in his ears when writing *Curlew River. Photo* Rosamund Strode.

332 *Curlew River.* The Rehearsal Score, by Imogen Holst, was published in 1965 with a cover designed by Berthold Wolpe. The work is dedicated to Michael Tippett 'in friendship and admiration'. This score was among the first publications issued by the new music publishing department of Faber & Faber.

333 *Orford Church, Suffolk. Curlew River*, with Peter Pears as the Madwoman and Bryan Drake as the Traveller – a production photograph from 1964. *Photo* Dominic.

334 Michael Tippett, 1957. Tippett was an old friend and colleague, about whom Britten wrote on the occasion of Tippett's sixtieth birthday in 1965: 'We have known each other now for more than twenty years; we have been very close often, at other times we have seemed to be moving in different directions. But whenever I see our two names bracketed together (and they often are, I am glad to say) I am reminded of the spirit of courage and integrity, sympathy, gaiety and profound musical independence which is yours, and I am proud to call you my friend.'

335-6 *Ghent, Belgium, 1967*. Pictures from a recital. *Photos* A. de Baenst, Ghent.
337-9 *Orford Church, Suffolk, 1967*. Rehearsals for the gramophone recording of *The Burning Fiery Furnace*, Op.77, the second of the Church Parables.
337 Britten, conducting.
338 Britten and Cecil Aronowitz, the viola player, who was later to be appointed the first director of string studies at the Britten-Pears school for Advanced Musical Studies at Snape.
339 Britten and Osian Ellis, the harpist. *Photos* Richard Adeney.

340 *Snape, 1967.* The Maltings. *Photo* John Donat.

341 *Snape, 2 June 1967.* The Queen, accompanied by the Duke of Edinburgh, comes to open The Maltings Concert Hall at Snape. *Photo* Clive Strutt.

342 The programme for the Inaugural Concert signed by the three Artistic Directors of the Festival.

THE TWENTIETH ALDEBURGH FESTIVAL OF MUSIC AND THE ARTS

In the Gracious Presence of Her Majesty the Queen
and His Royal Highness the Prince Philip, Duke of Edinburgh

THE INAUGURAL CONCERT

On the occasion of the opening of The Maltings Concert Hall, Snape
on Friday, June the 2nd 1967 at 3.15 pm

HEATHER HARPER *soprano*   PETER PEARS *tenor*   PHILIP JONES *trumpet*   KEITH HARVEY *cello*   PHILIP LEDGER *organ*
A chorus of East Anglian choirs   THE ALDEBURGH FESTIVAL SINGERS   THE BROADLAND SINGERS *Norwich*
THE CANTATA SINGERS *Ipswich*   THE LANTERN SINGERS *Lowestoft*   THE SUFFOLK SINGERS
THE WOLSEY CONSORT *Ipswich*   THE UNIVERSITY OF EAST ANGLIA CHOIR
THE ENGLISH CHAMBER ORCHESTRA   *Leader* EMANUEL HURWITZ
Conducted by BENJAMIN BRITTEN *and* IMOGEN HOLST

THE NATIONAL ANTHEM *arranged for chorus and orchestra by Benjamin Britten (born 1913)*

OVERTURE (WITH CHORUS) 'THE BUILDING OF THE HOUSE' *Op. 79, by Benjamin Britten*
First performance
I wrote this true example of Occasional Music during December and January of the past winter. It was certainly inspired by
the excitement of the planning and building—and the haste! I wanted to find a suitable text, and to fit it to music singable by an
amateur chorus with a professional orchestra. Imogen Holst suggested the text from *The Scottish Psalter*, and the old chorale
tune which Bach loved to use. B. B.
The words are printed overleaf

SUMMER NIGHT ON THE RIVER *for small orchestra by Frederick Delius (1862-1934)*
Delius was born in England but was, in fact, of Dutch extraction and never lived in England after his twentieth year. Yet to
many of us his music evokes the English landscape more vividly than any other composer's (except perhaps Grainger's—the
Australian living in U.S.A.!). This short piece, written in 1911, could easily be a tone-painting of the River Alde with its
rustling reeds, and its winds sighing over the marshes.

ST. PAUL'S SUITE *for string orchestra by Gustav Holst (1874-1934)*
1. Jig   2. Ostinato   3. Intermezzo   4. Finale: The Dargason
This suite was written in 1913 for the orchestra at St. Paul's Girls' School, where Holst taught for nearly thirty years.
Audiences have sometimes wondered how schoolgirls could have managed to play such an adventurous work as long ago as that.
It is true that the quickest passages were often a bit hectic and the highest notes were not always in tune. But Holst's music for
amateurs sounds equally at home when played by learners in a schoolroom or by professionals in a concert hall.

ODE FOR ST. CECILIA'S DAY *for soprano, tenor, chorus, organ and orchestra*
by George Frideric Handel (1685-1759)
On November the 22nd 1739 today's work, together with Handel's repeatedly successful setting of Dryden's other ode,
Alexander's Feast, was given at the Theatre Royal in Lincoln's Inn Fields. Performed six times that season, it enhanced both
poet's and composer's reputations, and the 'sublime majesty of the final chorus' was called 'worthy of Michael Angelo himself'.
The words of Dryden's poem are printed overleaf

341
342

343-50 In September 1967 at Long Melford Church, Suffolk, a performance of Bach's *Christmas Oratorio*, conducted by Britten, was recorded for BBC-TV. All the photographs belong to these sessions and were taken by Jack Phipps. In No. 345 can be seen the face of the principal cellist, Bernard Richards, who was a student friend of Britten at the Royal College in the 1930s.

351 Dennis Brain (1921-1957). In his memorial tribute to Brain, Britten wrote: 'I first met Dennis in the early summer of 1942 . . . . We soon became friends, and it took him no time at all to persuade me to write a special work for him. This turned out to be the *Serenade* for tenor, horn and strings, the première of which he and Peter Pears gave in 1943. His help was invaluable in writing the work; but he was always most cautious in advising any alterations. Passages which seemed impossible even for his prodigious gifts were practised over and over again before any modifications were suggested, such was his respect for a composer's ideas. He of course performed the work on many occasions, and for a period it seemed that no one else would ever be able to play it adequately. But, as usually happens when there is a work to play and a master who can play it, others slowly develop the means of playing it too, through his example. I must be grateful to Dennis for having challenged all other horn players in his playing of this piece. Some of my happiest musical experiences were conducting this work for him and Peter Pears – a succession of wonderful performances progressing from the youthful exuberance and brilliance of the early days to the maturity and deep understanding of the last few years.' (From *Tempo*, No.46, Winter, 1957-8, pp.5-6.)

352 James Blades playing the tubular bells (1970). His association with Britten was a long one and Jimmy not only took part in a great number of Britten premières but also acted as the composer's percussion consultant. Jimmy writes in his autobiography, *Drum Roll* (London, 1977): 'It was at a film session in that summer [1936] that I first met Benjamin Britten, and as I played the percussion parts, so ably written and conducted by the slim, shy young man who, at the time, was to me – and the rest of the small orchestra – just a newcomer, I little thought that here was the musician who would subsequently exercise the greatest influence on my career. One thing I vividly remember about that day at the G.P.O. Studios at Blackheath working on the film *Night Mail* is the fact that every member of the orchestra (of somewhat blasé session men) which Henry Bronkhurst had assembled for the occasion, found plenty to keep them busy and interested in young B.B.'s score.'

353 Percy Grainger (1882-1961). Date and place of this hitherto unpublished photograph unknown. Britten was an ardent admirer of Grainger and allotted his music a special place at the Aldeburgh Festival. His last orchestral work, the Suite on English Folk Tunes, Op.90 (1974), was 'lovingly and reverently dedicated' to Grainger's

memory. Grainger was, in fact, a very old love. We find Britten writing as a student in his diary on 3 March 1933 after listening to the radio: '. . . two brilliant folk-song arrangements of Percy Grainger – 17 come Sunday, & Father & Son, knocking all the V. Williams and R.O. Morris arrangements into a cocked-hat.'

354 *Aldeburgh, 1974.* Julian Bream (lute) and Peter Pears. A famous partnership. Britten wrote his *Nocturnal*, Op.70, for solo guitar, for Bream in 1963 and for the Pears/Bream voice/guitar duo he composed the *Songs from the Chinese*, Op.58, in 1957. *Photo* Victor Parker, New York.

355 *Aldeburgh, 1977.* The pianist, Sir Clifford Curzon. An old friend of the composer, and frequent visitor to Aldeburgh. In his contribution to the symposium published for Britten's fiftieth birthday he wrote: '. . . I wish I could find words of my own to describe the unique impression of your superb piano-playing; but it seems to defy all ordinary analysis. The complete mastery with which you dispose amounts and kinds of orchestrally-inspired tone would be as difficult for me to describe as Beethoven's volcanic playing apparently was for *his* contemporaries (if we are to judge by their rather shadowy accounts).' ('Twenty Years Ago', in *Tribute to Benjamin Britten*, pp.67-8.) (*See also No.174.*) *Photo* Nigel Luckhurst.

356 *Aldeburgh, 1972.* A rehearsal for the performance of Schumann's *Faust* at The Maltings on 11 June. On the left Jennifer Vyvyan; on

the right Dietrich Fischer-Dieskau, for whom Britten wrote his *Songs and Proverbs of William Blake*, Op.74, in 1965. In September 1972 Britten recorded the complete *Faust* for Decca. It was the last recording – certainly the last major recording – he made. *Photo* Jane Jacomb-Hood.

357 John Tooley, the General Administrator of the Royal Opera House, Covent Garden. He was appointed in 1970, since when the following first or new productions of operas by Britten have been mounted at the Royal Opera House: *Owen Wingrave* (1973), *Death in Venice* (1974) and *Peter Grimes* (1975). *Photo* Clive Barda.

358 *Aldeburgh, 1972.* Ralph Downes, the organist. *Photo* Jane Jacomb-Hood.

359 *Royal Opera House, Covent Garden, 1974.* James Bowman as Oberon in *A Midsummer Night's Dream*, with Julian Littman (Puck). *Photo* Reg Wilson.

360 *Royal Opera House, Covent Garden, 1974.* John Shirley-Quirk as the Gondolier in *Death in Venice*, with Peter Pears (Aschenbach). *Photo* John Garner.

361 *The Maltings, 3 June 1972.* On stage, left to right, are George Malcolm the harpsichordist, Joyce Grenfell and Max Adrian, who were rehearsing a programme of music and verse. *Photo* Jane Jacomb-Hood.

356 · 357 · 358
359 · 360 · 361

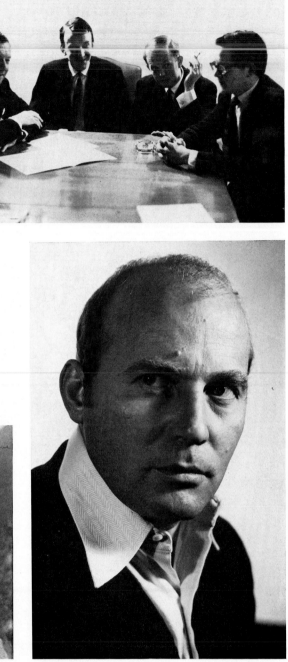

362 Sir William Walton (*b.* 1902). A portrait from the 1930s. *See No.78*, where Britten accompanied Sophie Wyss in a 1936 broadcast performance of two songs from *Façade* by Walton.

363 Dmitri Shostakovitch (1906-1975). An inscribed portrait from 1964. The dedication reads: 'To dear Benjamin Britten One of my most beloved composers With best wishes D. Shostakovitch 14.X.1964 Moscow'.

364 *London, 1963.* A Macnaghten Concert in honour of Britten's fiftieth birthday at the Mahatma Gandhi Hall, 25 October, when a work which had been composed by three of Britten's younger con-temporaries, Richard Rodney Bennett, Nicholas Maw and Malcolm Williamson (now Master of the Queen's Music) was given its first performance. In this photograph Britten talks to the three composers of *Reflections*: left to right, Bennett, Williamson and Maw.

365 Hans Werner Henze (*b.* 1926), the German composer. His *El Cimmaron* was given its world première at The Maltings on 22 June 1970. Britten's *Children's Crusade*, Op.82 (1968), is dedicated to Henze. Henze was composing his fifth string quartet in 1976 when news of Britten's death reached him, and the work is inscribed to Britten's memory. *Photo* José Verdeo, Mexico City.

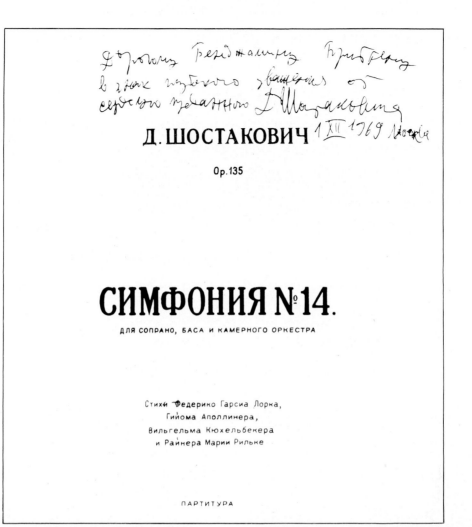

Д. ШОСТАКОВИЧ

Ор. 135

СИМФОНИЯ №14.

ДЛЯ СОПРАНО, БАСА И КАМЕРНОГО ОРКЕСТРА

Стихи Федерико Гарсиа Лорка,
Гийома Аполлинера,
Вильгельма Кюхельбекера
и Райнера Марии Рильке

ПАРТИТУРА

366 The title-page of Shostakovitch's Fourteenth Symphony which was dedicated to Britten. The score sent to Britten was inscribed thus in Shostakovitch's hand: 'To dear Benjamin Britten as a token of profound respect from a cordially devoted D. Shostakovitch. I XII 1969 Moscow'. It was to the Russian composer that Britten dedicated his third Church Parable, *The Prodigal Son* (1968).

367 *Moscow, probably March 1963*. Left to right: the former Director of the Bolshoi Theatre (Mr Chulaki, now retired), Rostropovitch, Britten, Shostakovitch, David Oistrakh and Rudolf Barshai (now in Israel). (*See also No. 313*.) *Photo* E. I. Iavno.
368 *Snape, 14 June 1970*. Britten rehearses Galina Vishnevskaya and Mark Rezhetin in Shostakovitch's Fourteenth Symphony. This was the first performance of the work outside Russia. *Photo* Jack Phipps.

369 *Snape, February 1969.* John Culshaw (the producer), Britten (who conducted) and Peter Pears (in costume as Grimes), during the recording of *Peter Grimes* for BBC-TV at The Maltings. The opera was first screened on BBC-2 on 2 November 1969. (Before he joined the BBC, John Culshaw had been responsible for the major series of Britten recordings issued by Decca.)

370 Heather Harper as Ellen Orford in the BBC-TV production of *Peter Grimes.*

371 *London, St Paul's Cathedral, 18 May 1969.* Britten with the Wandsworth School Choir at a rehearsal the day before the first performance of his *Children's Crusade,* Op.82. The work is inscribed: 'Written for the members of Wandsworth School Boys' Choir (musical director Russell Burgess) to perform on the 50th Anniversary of The Save the Children Fund at St Paul's Cathedral, May 19th 1969'.

372 Britten, thinking.
373 *Snape, 8 June 1969*. The Maltings after the fire on the first day
(7 June) of the 1969 Aldeburgh Festival. *Photo* Clive Strutt.

374 *Snape, 8 June 1969.* Britten and Pears amidst the ruins. *Photo* Clive Strutt.

375 *New York, The Essex House, October 1969.* Britten and Pears who gave concerts in New York and Boston in aid of the reconstruction of The Maltings. *Photo* © Jack Mitchell, New York.

376 *Snape, 21 November 1969.* The re-Building of the House. *Photo* Rosamund Strode.

377 The Countess of Cranbrook, Chairman of the Aldeburgh Festival Association from 1948, with Beth Reiss, wife of Stephen Reiss. An informal snap taken in the garden of The Red House. The *Cantata Misericordium*, Op.69, is dedicated to Lady Cranbrook.

378 *1967.* Stephen Reiss, General Manager of the Aldeburgh Festival (1956-1971). He is seen here at Snape in the year when The Maltings was opened. He won everybody's admiration for his resourcefulness when the disastrous fire of 1969 left him with a Festival on his hands, but no concert hall. *A Midsummer Night's Dream*, Op.64, is dedicated to him.

379 *Snape, 1970.* The Queen attends the opening concert of the Festival in the rebuilt Maltings.

380 *Suffolk, May 1970.* Britten and Pears (and the dog, Gilda) bird-watching and hoping to catch the song of an early nightingale in a Suffolk wood. *Photo* Rosamund Strode.

381 *The Maltings, Snape, November 1970.* Britten among the cameras. He is conducting the BBC-TV recording of *Owen Wingrave*, Op.85 (1970), commissioned for television by the BBC and first screened on 16 May 1971.

382 *Aldeburgh.* The Red House from the garden. *Photo* Jack Phipps.
383 *Aldeburgh, 1974.* The Red House. Hansjürg and Sally Lange with two of their children, Lars (on left) and Sven. Sally, Britten's niece, is the daughter of his sister Beth. *Photo* Rita Thomson.
384 *Aldeburgh, August 1968.* Sue Phipps, niece of Peter Pears and concert manager to Pears and Britten since 1965, with her new-born son, Martin Benjamin Peter, and one of his godfathers, in the garden of The Red House. (The other godfather is Peter Pears.) *Photo* Jack Phipps.

385 *October, 1971.* Britten and Verdi, a photograph by John Piper. Britten visited Venice in the company of the Pipers when work on *Death in Venice* was under way.

386 *Blythburgh Church, Suffolk, 13 November 1971.* Britten and Pears recording for BBC-TV Canticle IV, *Journey of the Magi,* Op.86, a setting of the poem by T.S. Eliot for counter-tenor (James Bowman, *see No.359*), tenor, baritone (John Shirley-Quirk, *see No.360*) and piano. The film was screened on BBC-2 on 12 December.

387 *Leningrad, 18 April 1971.* Britten is applauded after a performance of one of his works – the *Simple Symphony?* – by the conductorless Leningrad Chamber Orchestra. It is the leader, Lazar Gozman (now in the USA), who is presenting the composer to the public.

388 The Library at The Red House. This was often used for working, rehearsing, meetings and entertaining. It was here that Britten heard his last String Quartet for the first time when the Amadeus Quartet, for whom it was written, rehearsed it in his presence and finally played it through to the composer on 28/29 September 1976. (*See No.431.*) He did not live to hear the first performance of the work which took place at The Maltings on 19 December. *Photo* Nigel Luckhurst.

389 The Studio at Halliford Street (*see No.168*), London. *Photo* Jack Phipps.

390 Britten's Studio at Horham (*see No.399*). On the walls: top left, a drawing of Erwin Stein (by Milein Cosman); below it, a daguerreotype of Chopin; on the right, Frank Bridge. Not in view are portraits of Mozart and Mahler. *Photo* Nigel Luckhurst.

391-2 *Snape, 26 September 1971.* Pears sings for the first time at The Maltings Britten's Soutar songs, *Who are these children?*, Op.84 (No.392). At the same concert Britten took part in a performance of Mozart's G minor Piano Quartet (K.478) with the English Chamber Orchestra Ensemble. No.391 shows him rehearsing the work with (left to right) Kenneth Sillito (violin), Cecil Aronowitz

Starting slowly but animating
145
Tpt Trb
188
Tpt. 1
pp
cresc
Trb. 2
mp
Tpt. 2
Str ww
mf mellow
Trb 1
molto rall
Very slow
Aschenbach (realising the truth at last)
(almost spoken)
love you
Hn 2
pp
Horns
pizz
Vl. Vc.
p espress
189
long pause
(Vla Vc)
Hn
Db. Fg
Db
Fg
From Start of 189

(viola) and Kenneth Heath (cello). Rosamund Strode turns the pages. *Photos* Jack Phipps.

393 *Death in Venice*. A page from the composition sketch which shows the end of Act I and the beginning of Act II (Fig.189). Note the unbroken musical continuity of Britten's thought. At this stage he did not indicate the division between the acts.

394 *Aldeburgh, 17 December 1972*. The last page of *Death in Venice*, in Britten's MS composition sketch. The second date in brackets (24th) indicates that while the work had been effectively completed on the 17th, he continued to think about the orchestral epilogue and wrote out his final version of it on the 24th.

395 *Aldeburgh, June 1973*. The failing Aschenbach (Peter Pears) at the end of Act II responds to the final summons from Tadzio (Robert Huguenin). The first performance of the opera was given at The Maltings on 16 June 1973. The composer was not present – he was convalescing at Horham – nor had he been able to attend any of the rehearsals. *Photo* Nigel Luckhurst.

396 An aerial view of Schloss Wolfsgarten, Langen, Germany, the home of the Prince and Princess of Hesse, where Britten was a frequent visitor. It was here that he worked on *Death in Venice* in the spring of 1972.

397 *Schloss Wolfsgarten*. Britten and Pears sight-reading Schubert piano duets – an impromptu performance on the occasion of the birthday of Princess Margaret on 18 March 1973. This is the last photograph taken of Britten playing the piano. In May, he was to undergo open heart surgery at the National Heart Hospital, London.

398 *Schloss Wolfsgarten, October 1974*. At this time the USA première of *Death in Venice* was being given at the Metropolitan Opera, New York, and the trip to Germany did something to console Britten for not being able to travel to the States. On his knee he has the sketch-book for the Suite for orchestra on English Folk Tunes, Op.90, 'A time there was . . .', which was completed in November. *Photo* Dr Walter Otto.

396
397

399 *Horham, Suffolk, in the Spring.* Chapel House was bought in 1970 as a refuge from noisy aircraft over Aldeburgh and from the pressures surrounding The Red House; and during the last years of Britten's life was much used by him. The view across the field meant a great deal to him. It was *Owen Wingrave* that initiated the long series of late works substantially composed at Horham. *Photo* Rita Thomson.

400 *Horham, Spring 1976.* Britten in his chair outside the house and enjoying the view. *Photo* Rita Thomson.

401 *Horham, 1974.* Britten and Pears with Murray Perahia, the pianist. After his operation in 1973, Britten was no longer able to accompany Pears. Britten encouraged him to give recitals with Perahia and also with Osian Ellis, the harpist. (*See No.411.*) *Photo* Rita Thomson.

402 *Horham.* Chair and view in 1977. *Photo* Nigel Luckhurst.

403 *Sussex, Summer 1974.* A holiday photograph taken when Britten and Rita Thomson, his nurse, were staying with the Mitchells at Barcombe Mills. This picnic was on the Downs near Friston, not far from the house where Britten had stayed so often with the Bridges in his youth. Left to right: Britten, Kathleen Mitchell and Donald Mitchell. *Photo* Rita Thomson.

404-5 *Spring 1975.* Despite Britten's disabilities, he continued from time to time to take a carefully planned holiday at home and sometimes even abroad. These photographs were taken on a canal trip in Oxfordshire in a narrow boat, the *Amelia di Liverpool,* whose owners were the Shirley-Quirks. (*See No.360.*) Britten's armchair from The Red House was taken on board and placed at the prow. It was a trip the composer greatly enjoyed. In No.404 Peter Pears is at the helm. *Photo* Rita Thomson.

406 *Venice, November 1975*. Britten (with Rita Thomson, barely visible) on the balcony of his room at the Hotel Danieli. *Photo* William Servaes.

407 *Venice, 18 November 1975*. Britten and William Servaes, the General Manager of the Aldeburgh Festival since 1971. Britten made a final trip to Venice, a city he loved profoundly, accompanied by William and Pat Servaes and Rita Thomson. He took with him his wheelchair which enabled him, with the help of his friends, to be comparatively mobile and visit many old loves among palaces, buildings, galleries and gardens. This photograph was taken on Torcello. It was in Venice on this visit that he completed the sketch (16 November) of his third String Quartet, Op.94, the last movement of which uses material from *Death in Venice*. (*See No.431*.) Thus was brought to an end an historic series of working visits to a city by which he was always profoundly stirred. There can be no doubt that Britten's fascination with the place was at least one of the motives that also prompted his interest in Mann's novel, *Death in Venice*, as a theatrical subject. (*See Nos.393-5*.) *Photo* Rita Thomson.

408 Rita Thomson and Britten. Rita Thomson was a Sister at the National Heart Hospital, London, where Britten had his operation in 1973. In 1974, because of the highly delicate and problematic state of his health, she agreed to join the household at Aldeburgh and nurse him privately, full-time. Her professional skill and personal devotion meant that he was able to work – which for him was to live – up to the very last weeks of his life. *Photo* Beth Welford.

409 *Snape, 11 June 1976.* The South Bar at The Maltings where Britten is presented with a Citation of Honour by the Dean of the Faculty of Music of McGill University, Montreal. To the left of Professor Helmut Blume stands Rita Thomson. *Photo* Nigel Luckhurst.

410 *Aldeburgh, 13 June 1975.* The Queen Mother, Patron of the Aldeburgh Festival, arrives at The Red House for lunch and is greeted by Britten. This was the day of the first performance at The Maltings of Britten's Suite on English Folk Tunes, for orchestra. *Photo* Nigel Luckhurst.

411 *Snape, 17 June 1976.* Pears and Osian Ellis, in rehearsal. Britten was much impressed by the possibilities offered by the relatively unexploited voice-and-harp duo and was stimulated to write a num-

ber of late works for Pears and Ellis, among them Canticle V, Op.89 (1974), *The Death of St Narcissus* (T.S. Eliot); *A Birthday Hansel,* Op.92 (1975), the Burns song-cycle composed at the Queen's request for her mother's seventy-fifth birthday, which was being performed on this occasion; and a fresh batch of folksong settings (1976). He also rearranged some of his earlier voice and piano folksong settings for the new duo. *Photo* Nigel Luckhurst.

412 *Snape, 16 June 1976.* Robert Lowell (1917-1977), the American poet, and Caroline Blackwood. It was Lowell's version of Racine's *Phèdre* that Britten used in *Phaedra*, Op.93, the dramatic cantata for mezzo-soprano and small orchestra he wrote for Dame Janet Baker. For the occasion of the first performance, Lowell travelled to Aldeburgh and met Britten during the interval. They had met only once previously, in New York in 1969. *Photo* Nigel Luckhurst.

413 *Thorpeness, Suffolk, June 1976.* A rehearsal at the Working Men's Hall of Britten's cantata, *Phaedra.* Behind Dame Janet and Britten stands Colin Matthews, the composer, who was the principal editor of Britten's music during the composer's last years and assisted him with the preparation of the full score of the *Welcome Ode*, Op.95, for young people's chorus and orchestra, his last complete work. *Photo* Nigel Luckhurst.

414 *Snape, June 1976.* Rehearsing *Phaedra*. Left to right: Dame Janet, Britten, and Steuart Bedford, who conducted the first performance. Bedford has been responsible for many important Britten premières, including the first performance of *Death in Venice* and the first stage performance of *Owen Wingrave*. *Photo* Nigel Luckhurst.

415 *Snape, June 1976.* A rehearsal of *Our Hunting Fathers*, Op.8, at The Maltings. Left to right: Pears, André Previn (who conducted), Britten and Elisabeth Söderström (the soloist). *Photo* Nigel Luckhurst.

416 *Jubilee Hall, Aldeburgh, 1976.* Britten and Rostropovitch. Britten wrote no less than five major works for Rostropovitch, not to speak of the Pushkin songs (*The Poet's Echo*) for his wife (Galina) in which the cellist turned piano accompanist. *Photo* Nigel Luckhurst.

417 *Aldeburgh, probably 1975.* Leslie Periton and Britten watching the Aldeburgh Carnival. Periton was Britten's accountant for thirty-five years and a close friend, and is now an Executor of the Britten Estate. *Photo* Rita Thomson.

418 *Snape, June 1975.* Isador Caplan (left) talks to Colin Graham (right) at The Maltings. Isador Caplan was Britten's lawyer for thirty years and is one of the Executors of the Britten Estate. *Owen Wingrave* is dedicated to him and his wife, Joan. Colin Graham, the producer, worked closely with Britten from 1957 onwards and was responsible for a long list of major first productions of Britten's operas, among them *Noye's Fludde*, the three Church Parables, *Owen Wingrave* (on TV, with Brian Large) and *Death in Venice*.

He became an Artistic Director of the Aldeburgh Festival in 1969 and was resident producer of the English Opera Group from 1964. When the Group was transformed, in 1975, into the English Music Theatre, he became an Artistic Director and chief producer of the new company. He was also author of the libretto of Britten's Vaude-ville for boys and piano, *The Golden Vanity*, Op.78 (1966). *Photo Nigel Luckhurst.*

419 *The Red House, Aldeburgh, 20 May 1976.* Britten and Pears photographed during the making of a Thames Television programme, 'Musical Triangles'.

lizabeth the Second by the Grace of God OF THE UNITED KINGDOM OF GREAT BRITAIN AND NORTHERN IRELAND AND OF OUR OTHER REALMS AND TERRITORIES QUEEN HEAD OF THE COMMONWEALTH, DEFENDER OF THE FAITH To all Lords Spiritual & Temporal & all other Our Subjects whatsoever to whom these Presents shall come Greeting Know Ye that We of Our special grace certain knowledge and mere motion in pursuance of the Life Peerages Act 1958 & of all other powers in that behalf Us enabling do by these Presents advance create and prefer Our trusty and well beloved EDWARD BENJAMIN BRITTEN Esquire Member of Our Order of Merit Member of Our Order of the Companions of Honour to the state degree style dignity title and honour of BARON BRITTEN of Aldeburgh in Our County of Suffolk And for Us Our heirs & successors do appoint give & grant unto him the said name state degree style dignity title and honour of Baron Britten to have & to hold unto him for his life Willing and by these Presents granting for Us Our heirs & successors that he may have hold & possess a seat place and voice in the Parliaments and Public Assemblies and Councils of Us Our heirs & successors within Our United Kingdom amongst the Barons And also that he may enjoy and use all the rights privileges pre-eminences immunities and advantages to the degree of a Baron duly and of right belonging which Barons of Our United Kingdom have heretofore used and enjoyed or as they do at present use & enjoy In Witness whereof We have caused these Our Letters to be made Patent Witness Ourself at Westminster the second day of July in the twenty-fifth year of Our Reign

BY WARRANT UNDER THE QUEEN'S SIGN MANUAL

420 *Aldeburgh, 12 June 1976.* In The Red House garden. Britten and Donald Mitchell. *Photo* Nigel Luckhurst.
421 The Letters Patent bestowing on Britten the title of Baron Britten of Aldeburgh, in the County of Suffolk.

420
421

422 On Saturday 12 June 1976 it was made known that Britten had been created a Life Peer in the Queen's Birthday Honours. A party was given in the garden of The Red House to celebrate the event. Britten talks to Lady Cranbrook, Chairman of the Aldeburgh Festival. On Lady Cranbrook's left, at the back of the picture, stands Dr. Walter Otto who photographed Britten at Wolfsgarten. (*See No.398.*) Behind Britten is Lady Melville, wife of Sir Eugene Melville, Chairman of the Aldeburgh Festival-Snape Maltings Foundation, who stands on the right. Farthest right, Britten's sister, Beth. *Photo* Nigel Luckhurst.

423 *Aldeburgh, 12 June 1976.* Britten in the garden of The Red House with (left) Mrs Cooper, his housekeeper from 1972, and (right) Heather Bryson, who has helped in the house since 1962. *Photo* Rita Thomson.

424 *Aldeburgh, 12 June 1976.* The end of the party. The departing guests include (left to right) Jenni Vaulkhard, Charles Gifford, Letty Gifford (Mrs Charles Gifford, back to camera) and Joan Caplan. *Photo* Nigel Luckhurst.

422 · 423

425 *The Red House, Aldeburgh, 6 February 1976.* Britten in the drawing-room. *Photo* Nigel Luckhurst.

426 *Aldeburgh, The Red House, 15 April 1976.* Britten and Pears on the terrace outside the Library. *Photo* Nigel Luckhurst.

427 *Bergen, Norway, 1 July 1976.* Pears and Britten outside the Solstrand Fjord Hotel. This was the last overseas journey Britten was to make. It was undertaken as a holiday but, true to form to the last, it was here that Britten started work on a new composition, though he was never to finish it (*see No.439*). *Photo* Hans H. Rowe, Bergen.

428 Hans Keller (*b.* 1919) to whom Britten inscribed his last String Quartet. Keller had championed Britten's music since the late 1940s and edited (with Donald Mitchell) a symposium on Britten, published in 1952 (though already in the spring of 1950 the same editors had devoted an issue of their polemical 'little' review, *Music Survey*, to Britten's works). It was patient prodding from Keller over the years that helped keep the idea of a new String Quartet alive in the composer's mind.

429 *The Red House, Aldeburgh, 24 September 1976.* A last portrait of Britten and his hands. This photograph and No.430 below were taken without artificial light, as is Mrs Gaye's custom. The photo-

grapher was distressed to find her subject so frail, as a consequence of which 'the results were not as good as she had hoped because her own hands shook.' *Photo Bertl Gaye, Cambridge.*

430 The MS on which Britten's hands rest is a fair copy of the score of his third String Quartet made by Rosamund Strode. *Photo Bertl Gaye, Cambridge.*

431 A MS page from the composition sketch of Britten's third String Quartet. We show the opening of the last (fifth) movement, the Passacaglia, entitled 'La Serenissima' and incorporating material from *Death in Venice.*

432 *Aldeburgh, 7 December 1976.* Britten had died at home in the early hours of 4 December. The hearse passes through the town on its way to the Parish Church.

433-4 The coffin is followed by members of Britten's family (right to left): Robert Britten, his elder brother; the younger of his two sisters, Beth; and behind her, Barbara. Peter Pears and Rita Thomson walk together, followed by the Princess of Hesse, Hansjürg Lange and his wife (partly visible) and Rostropovitch.

BENJAMIN BRITTEN

Order of Merit · Companion of Honour
Baron Britten of Aldeburgh in the County of Suffolk

22nd November 1913, Lowestoft
4th December 1976, Aldeburgh

Freeman of the Boroughs of Lowestoft and Aldeburgh
Fellow of the Royal College of Music
Honorary Member of the Royal Academy of Music
Honorary Freeman of the Worshipful Company of Musicians
Honorary Doctor of Music in the Universities of
    Belfast, Cambridge, Nottingham, Hull, Oxford,
    Manchester, London, Leicester, East Anglia,
    Wales and Warwick,
Honorary Fellow of Magdalene College, Cambridge
Honorary Member of Worcester College, Oxford

Tuesday 7th December 1976, 2.30 pm

ALDEBURGH PARISH CHURCH
Vicar Rev Canon Geoffrey Oram

435 The procession to the grave is led by the Lord Bishop of St Edmundsbury and Ipswich, the Right Rev. Dr Leslie Brown, who concluded his address with these words: 'Ben will like the sound of the trumpets, though he will find it difficult to believe they are sounding for him.'

436 The Order of Service.

437 The burial. The grave had been lined with rushes gathered from the marshes at Snape by the caretaker of The Maltings, Bob Ling, and his wife Doris, both good friends of the composer.

438 *Aldeburgh Parish Church.* The grave. The gravestone was designed and carved by Reynolds Stone. *Photo* Rosamund Strode.

439 It was Edith Sitwell's poem 'Praise We Great Men' (*see No.302*) that Britten, during the last months of his life, began to set as a Cantata for solo quartet, chorus and orchestra. He had completed a significant portion of the projected work in sketch when his final illness overtook him. We reproduce the opening page of the short score of this last, incomplete composition which Britten had hoped to have ready for the opening concert of the 1977/78 season of the National Symphony Orchestra of Washington, D.C., which Rostropovitch was to conduct.

WESTMINSTER ABBEY

A

SERVICE OF THANKSGIVING

for the Life and Work of

BENJAMIN BRITTEN, O.M., C.H.

BARON BRITTEN OF ALDEBURGH IN THE
COUNTY OF SUFFOLK

Born 22 November 1913 Lowestoft
Died 4 December 1976 Aldeburgh

Thursday 10 March 1977

at 12 noon

Freeman of the Boroughs of Lowestoft and Aldeburgh
Fellow of the Royal College of Music
Honorary Member of the Royal Academy of Music
Honorary Freeman of the Worshipful Company of Musicians
Honorary Doctor of Music in the Universities of
 Belfast, Cambridge, Nottingham, Hull, Oxford, Manchester, London,
 Leicester, East Anglia, Wales and Warwick
Honorary Fellow of Magdalene College, Cambridge
Honorary Member of Worcester College, Oxford
Royal Philharmonic Society's Gold Medal, London (1964)
Commander of the Royal Order of the Pole Star, Sweden (1962)
Citation of Honour from McGill University, Montreal (1976)
Associé de l'Académie des Beaux-Arts, Paris (1976)

Honorary Member of the following:

BELGIUM
Académie Royale des Sciences, des Lettres, et des Beaux-Arts, Brussels
 (1955)
FEDERAL REPUBLIC OF GERMANY
Bayerischen Akademie der Schönen Künste, Munich (1972)
Akademie der Künste, Berlin (1959)
Akademie der Künste, Hamburg (1962)
GERMAN DEMOCRATIC REPUBLIC
Akadamie der Künste, Berlin
ITALY
Accademia Nazionale Cherubini, Florence (1955)
Accademia Nazionale di Santa Cecilia, Rome (1958)
Accademia Musicale Chigiana, Siena
SWEDEN
Svenska Musicaliska Academiens, Vagnar
U.S.A.
American Academy of Arts and Letters and the National Institute of Arts
 and Letters, New York (1960)
YUGOSLAVIA
Académie Serbe des Sciences et des Arts, Belgrade (1965)

Medals:
Coolidge Medal, New York (1941)
Mahler Medal of Honour, Bruckner and Mahler Society of America (1967)
Mozart Medal for 1976, Mozartgemeinde, Vienna

Prizes and Awards:
Hanseatic Goethe Prize, Hamburg (1961)
Aspen Award for Services to the Humanities, Colorado (1964)
Leonie Sonning Prize, Copenhagen (1968)
Wihuri-Sibelius Prize, Helsinki (1965)
Ernst von Siemens Prize, Munich (1973)
Maurice Ravel Prize, Paris (1974)

3

---

440 *London, 10 March 1977.* The Order Paper for the Service of Thanksgiving at Westminster Abbey, which also included a list of Britten's honours and decorations. The music included the Adagio from Schubert's String Quintet (*see No.276*) and Britten's Antiphon, Op.56b (1956); and works by Bach, Bridge, Mozart, Purcell and Malcolm Williamson. The address was given by The Very Reverend Walter Hussey, The Dean of Chichester, for whom *Rejoice in the Lamb*, Op.30, had been composed in 1943, the text of which was read during the Service by Peter Pears.

An asterisk indicates an illustration, the number of which appears in the right-hand column.

YEAR	EVENTS	COMPOSITIONS	ILLUSTRATIONS
1913	*22 November* Born at Lowestoft, 21 Kirkley Cliff Road*, the youngest child of Mr and Mrs R. V. Britten*. The eldest of the four children was Barbara (*b.* 1902) and Britten's older brother Robert and sister Elizabeth (Beth) were born respectively in 1907 and 1909.		11 4
c. 1918	First piano lessons from his mother, an active amateur singer and secretary of the Lowestoft Choral Society.	First compositions.	
c. 1921	Piano lessons with Miss Ethel Astle*, a local teacher at the pre-preparatory school he attended with the younger of his two sisters, Beth.		45
1922-3		Early piano compositions and songs, including 'Beware!'*	28-9
1923	Enters South Lodge Preparatory School*, Lowestoft, as a day boy.		34, 36
c. 1923	Viola lessons with Miss Audrey Alston* of Norwich.		74
1924	Hears Frank Bridge's orchestral suite, *The Sea*, at Norwich Triennial Festival.		
1925		Overture in B flat minor, for full orchestra.	
1926	Passes finals (Grade VIII) Associated Board piano examination with honours.		
1927	Hears Bridge's *Enter Spring* at Norwich and meets Bridge for the first time through Audrey Alston. Begins composition lessons* with Bridge in London and at Bridge's home at Friston*, near Eastbourne, during school holidays.		46, 50, 51 48
1927-8	Head Boy of South Lodge, captain of cricket* and *Victor Ludorum*.		31, 35
1928	*July* *September* Enters Gresham's School*, Holt. Continues composition lessons with Bridge; piano lessons with Harold Samuel* in London.	Settings of Hugo and Verlaine for soprano and orchestra.	41 47
1929	*June*	'The Birds' (Belloc song).	
1930	*July* Leaves Gresham's. Wins open scholarship to Royal College of Music*, London. *September* Enters Royal College of Music. Composition lessons with John Ireland*. Piano lessons with Arthur Benjamin*. Lodges initially at 51 Prince's Square, Bayswater, W.2. Later moves to room at 173 Cromwell Road, S.W.5*, where his sister Beth also lodges.	*Hymn to the Virgin.*	60 58 62 65
1931	*May-June* *July* Wins Ernest Farrar Prize (£7!) for composition.	String Quartet in D major (unpublished until 1975).	
1932-3	Active association with Macnaghten-Lemare concerts of new music at Ballet Club Theatre (later known as Mercury Theatre).	Three Two-part Songs (de la Mare).	
1932	*9 July* *October*	*Sinfonietta*, Op. 1. *Phantasy Quartet*, Op. 2.	

YEAR	EVENTS	COMPOSITIONS	ILLUSTRATIONS
1936	*April* To Barcelona for ISCM Festival where Antonio Brosa plays Violin Suite, Op. 6 (broadcast first on 6 March*).		78
	July Spanish Civil War begins.		
	23 July	*Our Hunting Fathers**, Op. 8 (with Auden).	88
		Soirées Musicales, Op. 9.	
1937	Composed music for *Love from a Stranger*, his only feature film.	GPO: *Calendar of the Year* and *The Line to the Tschierva Hut*.	
		THEATRE: *The Ascent of F.6** (Auden and Isherwood) and *Out of the Picture* (MacNeice) (both Group Theatre).	102-3
		BBC: *The Company of Heaven* and *King Arthur**.	104
		FILM: *Love from a Stranger* (Trafalgar Films/Boyd Neel*, music director).	130
		Pacifist March (for Peace Pledge Union).	
		Four Cabaret Songs* (Auden, unpublished).	103
		Two Ballads (Slater and Auden).	
	18 January Britten's mother dies in London.		
	March Britten's friendship with Peter Pears begins.	*Variations on a Theme of Frank Bridge*, Op. 10.	
	12 July		
	27 August Bridge Variations performed at Salzburg Festival, conducted by Boyd Neel. Britten attends.		
	October	*On this Island*, Op. 11 (Auden texts).	
	Acquires Old Mill* at Snape, near Aldeburgh, Suffolk.	*Mont Juic**, Op. 12 (with Lennox Berkeley).	110, 85, 86
	November	*Fish in the Unruffled Lakes* (Auden).	
1938		GPO: *How the dial works*, *The Tocher* (Rossini arrangements).	
		THEATRE: *On the Frontier* (Auden and Isherwood/Group Theatre).	
		BBC: *Hadrian's Wall* (with Auden), *The Sword in the Stone*,	
		The World of the Spirit*.	93
	22 January Britten's sister, Beth, marries.		
	April Moves into Old Mill, Snape. Works at Piano Concerto.		
	26 July	Piano Concerto, Op. 13.	
	Autumn	*Advance Democracy* (Randall Swingler[1]/chorus *a cappella*).	
1939-42	Britten leaves UK with Pears, on a trip to N. America. They travel first to Canada, then move on to the USA, where they remain (principally in New York) until 1942. While in the United States Britten earns his living conducting (a semi-amateur orchestra in Long Island)*, touring (as soloist in his own Piano Concerto* and in recitals with Peter Pears), composing and arranging. (Some scores for Canadian and American radio were also written at this time.) He writes a College 'operetta' with W. H. Auden, *Paul Bunyan**, and is commissioned by Paul Wittgenstein* to write a work for piano (left hand) and orchestra, the *Diversions*, first performed on 16 January 1942 at Philadelphia.		139, 140 129
			142-143, 157
1939		GPO: *God's Chillun* (which started life as *Negroes*, with Auden as collaborator), *H.P.O.* or *6d. Telegram*.	
		FILM: *Advance Democracy* (Realist Film Unit).	
		THEATRE: *Johnson over Jordan* (J. B. Priestley).	
	19 January W. H. Auden and Christopher Isherwood leave UK for USA*.		112
	29 March	*Ballad of Heroes*, Op. 14 (Swingler and Auden).	

[1]Randall Swingler (1909-1967) was a prominent leftwing writer and poet. At the time of his collaborations with Britten he was on the staff of the then *Daily Worker* (whose literary editor he became). He was also the last editor of the *Left Review*. He was himself a gifted flautist and worked on various occasions with other composers, notably Alan Bush, Christian Darnton, Alan Rawsthorne and Bernard Stevens.

YEAR	EVENTS	COMPOSITIONS	ILLUSTRATIONS
1939	*May* or *June* Britten and Pears leave for N. America, first visiting Canada.		
	21 August They arrive in New York*, meet Dr and Mrs William Mayer* and their family, and take up residence with them on Long Island.		114
			119, 120
	3 September Second World War begins.		
	20 September	Violin Concerto*, Op. 15.	136, 137
	25 October	*Les Illuminations*, Op. 18.	
	10 December	*Canadian Carnival*, Op. 19.	
1940		*Sinfonia da Requiem*, Op. 20.	
	30 January First complete performance of *Les Illuminations* given in London*. Britten in USA.		131
	January and *February* Britten seriously ill in New York.		
	Summer	*Diversions*, Op. 21.	
	30 October The Michelangelo Sonnets were written for and dedicated to Peter Pears, the first vocal work specifically composed for him by Britten.	*Seven Sonnets of Michelangelo*, Op. 22.	
	November Britten and Pears move into 7 Middagh Street, Brooklyn Heights, and stay there until the summer of 1941.	*Introduction and Rondo alla Burlesca*, Op. 23, No. 1.	
1941		*Matinées Musicales*, Op. 24.	
	10 January Frank Bridge dies in Brighton.		
	5 May *Paul Bunyan* first performed at Columbia University, New York*.	*Paul Bunyan* (Op. 17, text by W. H. Auden; unpublished until 1978).	141, 144
	July	*Mazurka Elegiaca*, Op. 23, No. 2.	
		String Quartet No. 1, Op. 25.	
	Summer Trip to Escondido, California, where Britten and Pears stay with the piano duo, Ethel Bartlett and Rae Robertson, for whom Britten wrote a number of two-piano works*.		145-8
	Encounters poetry of George Crabbe.		
	September First performance of String Quartet No. 1 in Los Angeles. Britten awarded Library of Congress Medal for Services to Chamber Music.		
	27 October	*Scottish Ballad*, Op. 26.	
1942	Britten and Pears decide to return home to UK.		
	16 March Britten and Pears bid farewell to the Mayer family on Long Island*, leaving New York on the MS *Axel Johnson*, travelling up the coast to Halifax before the Atlantic crossing, arriving in the UK on 17 April. Britten brings home with him a commission from the Koussevitzky Foundation which is to be *Peter Grimes*, Britten having been further stimulated in the meantime to undertake this subject by reading Crabbe's 'The Borough'. He composes on the voyage* *Hymn to St Cecilia* (Auden), and *Ceremony of Carols*.		160
			159
1942-45	On return to the UK Britten appears before a tribunal as a committed conscientious objector and is exempted from military service (as is Pears). He continues with composing (some radio and incidental music still) and gives many wartime recitals with Pears* under the auspices of the Council for the Encouragement of Music and the Arts (CEMA) (the condition on which exemption was granted). They also give prison concerts. He lives at various addresses in London and also visits the Old Mill at Snape, ownership of which he has retained during his absence in the USA and which has been occupied by his sister Beth and her children (while her husband was on war service). It is here that he composes *Peter Grimes*.	*Hymn to St Cecilia*, Op. 27. *Ceremony of Carols*, Op. 28.	161
1943		BBC: *The Rescue* (E. Sackville-West).	
	May	*Prelude and Fugue*, Op. 29, for strings.	
	17 July	*Rejoice in the Lamb*, Op. 30.	

The *Serenade* was dedicated to Edward Sackville-West (1901-1965) who was an early and sympathetic writer about Britten's music after the composer's return from the States.
December

Serenade, Op. 31.

The Ballad of Little Musgrave and Lady Barnard.

1944 *8/9 November*
December

Festival Te Deum, Op. 32.
BBC: *A Poet's Christmas* (setting of Auden text, 'A Shepherd's Carol', unpublished until 1962).

1945

THEATRE: *This way to the tomb* (R. Duncan/Mercury Theatre).

February Peter Grimes completed (at Snape)*.
7 May Germany surrenders.
7 June First performance of *Peter Grimes** at Sadler's Wells, London.
Summer Visit to Belsen and other concentration camps as Menuhin's accompanist.
19 August
14 October

Peter Grimes, Op. 33.   181 / 185-7

Holy Sonnets of John Donne, Op. 35.
String Quartet No. 2, Op. 36.

1946

THEATRE: *Duchess of Malfi* (Webster/Brecht, etc.), New York; *The Eagle has two heads* (Cocteau/Duncan).

21 January

BBC: *The Dark Tower** (MacNeice).   210-11

Spring
Summer Post-war Glyndebourne reopens on 12 July with first performance of *Lucretia** conducted by Ansermet. The production was then taken on tour, setting an annual pattern for the future, especially after the English Opera Group, the organization of which was now under discussion, was launched. (See 1947.)
USA première of *Peter Grimes* at Tanglewood, Mass.*

The Rape of Lucretia, Op. 37.

188-204

205-9

This film was first shown on 29 November. It had been preceded by the first concert performance of the work on 15 October, conducted by Malcolm Sargent.

Prelude and Fugue on a Theme of Vittoria.
FILM: *Instruments of the Orchestra* (*Young Person's Guide*, Op. 34).

1947 *20 July* The newly formed English Opera Group* gives the first performance of *Albert Herring** at Glyndebourne, Britten conducting.
Britten buys a house in Aldeburgh: Crag House*, 4 Crabbe Street; and lives there for ten years.
Summer Britten, Pears and Eric Crozier* propose to organize a Festival at Aldeburgh.
12 September
Christmas

Albert Herring, Op. 39.   212 / 214

227, 228

221

Canticle I, Op. 40.
A Charm of Lullabies, Op. 41.
BBC: *Men of Goodwill.*

1948 *May*
24 May First performance of *The Beggar's Opera** at the Arts Theatre, Cambridge, Britten conducting.
June First Aldeburgh Festival* opens with the first performance in the Parish Church of *St Nicolas*, Leslie Woodgate conducting.

The Beggar's Opera, Op. 43.   222

St Nicolas, Op. 42.   224

1949 *April*
14 June First performance of *Let's make an Opera* at the Jubilee Hall, Aldeburgh, Norman Del Mar conducting*.
June
9 July The *Spring Symphony* was first performed at the Holland Festival, Eduard van Beinum conducting the Concertgebouw Orchestra*. Britten's music was much performed at successive Holland Festivals, particularly during the régime of Peter Diamand.

The Little Sweep, Op. 45.

Spring Symphony, Op. 44.   238

245-6

THEATRE: *Stratton* (Duncan).

Autumn North American recital tour* with Pears, returning to the UK in December.

A Wedding Anthem, Op. 46.   243

YEAR	EVENTS	COMPOSITIONS	ILLUSTRATIONS
1950	*February* Starts work on *Billy Budd*, with E. M. Forster and Eric Crozier as librettists*.		250
		Five Flower Songs, Op. 47.	
	April	*Lachrymae*, Op. 48a (see also 1976).	
1951	Festival of Britain.	*Six Metamorphoses after Ovid*, Op. 49.	
	1 May First performance of Purcell's *Dido and Aeneas*, realized and edited by Britten and Imogen Holst*, who was later to become Britten's music assistant.		287
	Summer Receives Freedom of the Borough of Lowestoft*.		247
	Autumn	*Billy Budd*, Op. 50.	
	1 December *Billy Budd*, an Arts Council Festival production, first performed at Covent Garden, Britten conducting*.		252, 254
1952	*January*	*Canticle II*, Op. 51*.	249
	Spring Starts work on *Gloriana*, with libretto by William Plomer*.		257
	Imogen Holst joins Britten as his music assistant.*		284
	October First television production of a Britten opera: *Billy Budd*, by NBC-TV (USA)*.		253
1953	Created CH in the Coronation Honours List.		
	13 March	*Gloriana*, Op. 53.	
	8 June First performance of *Gloriana** at Covent Garden. Gala performance as part of Coronation celebrations of Queen Elizabeth II.		255, 256
	September	*Winter Words*, Op. 52.	
	Autumn Starts work on *The Turn of the Screw*, with libretto by Myfanwy Piper.		
1954		*The Turn of the Screw*, Op. 54.	
	14 September First performance of *The Turn of the Screw*, at Teatro la Fenice, Venice, Britten conducting*. Apart from *Paul Bunyan*, the only occasion on which the première of a Britten opera was given overseas.		262, 265
	November	*Canticle III*, Op. 55 (poem by Edith Sitwell)*.	303
1955	Concerts with Pears in Belgium and Switzerland, followed by two weeks ski-ing holiday, when the *Alpine Suite*, for recorder trio, was written.	*Alpine Suite* and *Scherzo* (both for recorders).	
	February English Opera Group overseas tour of *The Turn of the Screw*.	*Hymn to St Peter*, Op. 56a.	
	November Towards the end of the year, Britten and Pears leave on world tour, part of it in company of the Prince and Princess of Hesse*. The trip took in Austria, Yugoslavia, Turkey, Singapore, Indonesia (Java and Bali), Japan (Tokyo), Macau, Hong Kong, Thailand (Bangkok), India and Ceylon. Britten returns to UK in the middle of March. The musical consequences of the Far East trip were profound and far-reaching. The *Pagodas* ballet reflects the impact the Balinese *gamelan* made on Britten, while it was in Tokyo that he witnessed the Nõh play that some eight years later generated the composition of *Curlew River*, the first of the three Church Parables.		293-8
		Antiphon, Op. 56b.	
1956	*Summer* Holiday in Tarasp (Switzerland)*.		271, 275
	Autumn	*The Prince of the Pagodas*, Op. 57.	
	November German tour with Pears.		
1957	*1 January* First performance of full-length ballet, *The Prince of the Pagodas*, at Covent Garden, Britten conducting.		
	April Elected honorary member of the American Academy of Arts and Letters and of the National Institute of Arts and Letters, New York.		

YEAR	EVENTS	COMPOSITIONS	ILLUSTRATIONS
	Autumn	*Songs from the Chinese*, Op. 58.	
	August–October English Opera Group tour of Canada. Britten later visits Berlin Festival.		
	27 October Starts work on *Noye's Fludde*.		
	November Moves to The Red House*, Aldeburgh, where he lives until his death.		323
	December	*Noye's Fludde*, Op. 59.	
1958	*The Story of Music* published: co-author, Imogen Holst.		
	18 June First performance of *Noye's Fludde** at Aldeburgh Festival.		299–301
	Summer	*Nocturne*, Op. 60.	
		Six Hölderlin Fragments, Op. 61.	
1959	*March*	*Cantata Academica*, Op. 62.	
	May	*Fanfare for St Edmundsbury.*	
		Missa Brevis, Op. 63.	
	Enlargement and improvement of Jubilee Hall, Aldeburgh. Visits Venice.		
	October Starts work on *A Midsummer Night's Dream*, with libretto by Pears and Britten (after Shakespeare).		
1960	*15 April*	*A Midsummer Night's Dream*, Op. 64.	
	11 June First performance of *A Midsummer Night's Dream* in reconstructed Jubilee Hall.		
	Revisions of *Billy Budd* (from four acts to two).		
	English Opera Group to be managed by Royal Opera House, Covent Garden.		
	September First meeting with Rostropovitch at Royal Festival Hall, London.		
	13 November BBC studio broadcast of revised version of *Billy Budd*.		
1961	*January*	Sonata in C, for cello and piano, Op. 65.	
	February	*Jubilate Deo* (for chorus and organ).	
	9 May	*Fancie* (Shakespeare song, for unison voices and piano).	
	7 July First performance of Cello Sonata at Jubilee Hall, Aldeburgh, by Rostropovitch and Britten*.		305–6
	20 December *War Requiem* completed.	*War Requiem*, Op. 66.	
1962	*1 May* *Psalm 150* was written for the centenary celebrations of Old Buckenham Hall School, formerly South Lodge School, Lowestoft.	*Psalm 150*, Op. 67, for two-part children's voices and instruments.	
	30 May First performance of *War Requiem* at rebuilt Coventry Cathedral, Meredith Davies and Britten conducting*.		312
	22 October Britten receives Honorary Freedom of the Borough of Aldeburgh*.		309–10
	29 December	*A Hymn of St Columba* (for chorus and organ).	
1963	*March* Britten and Pears participate in Festival of British Music in USSR, organized by British Council*.		313
	3 May	*Symphony for Cello and Orchestra*, Op. 68.	
		Night Piece (for piano).	
	25 May	*Cantata Misericordium*, Op. 69.	
	1 September First performance of *Cantata Misericordium* at Geneva, Ansermet conducting.		
	11 November		
	22 November Britten's fiftieth birthday was widely celebrated throughout the year. Among the principal events were an all-Britten Prom and a new production of *Peter Grimes* (by Basil Coleman) at Sadler's Wells, while *Gloriana* was revived in a concert performance at the Royal Festival Hall.	*Nocturnal*, Op. 70, for guitar.	

YEAR	EVENTS	COMPOSITIONS	ILLUSTRATIONS
1964	*February* Visits Venice to work on *Curlew River*.		
	12 March First performance of Cello Symphony in Moscow, with Rostropovitch as soloist and Britten conducting. During this same visit, *Peter Grimes* was performed for the first time in the USSR.		
	Maundy Thursday	*Curlew River*, Op. 71, A Parable for Church Performance*.	332
	Spring Visits Budapest, where he meets the twins for whom he is to write the *Gemini Variations*.		
	12 June First performance of *Curlew River** at Orford Church, Suffolk, which is then taken on tour by EOG at home and overseas.		333
	26 June First English performance of Cello Symphony*.		322
	July Travels to Aspen, Colorado, USA, to receive first Aspen Award on 31 July*.		315
	Britten travels with EOG on USSR tour with *Lucretia*, *Herring* and *The Turn of the Screw*.		
	November–December	Suite for Cello, Op. 72.	
1965	Britten is awarded the OM.		
	During this year the first publications of the newly established music division of Faber & Faber* appear, among them Britten's *Nocturnal* and *Curlew River*.		330, 332
	He visits India, where he starts work on the *Gemini Variations*.		
	March	*Gemini Variations*, Op. 73, quartet for two players.	
	6 April	*Songs and Proverbs of William Blake*, Op. 74.	
	July	*Voices for Today*, Op. 75 (Anthem for chorus).	
	August Armenian Holiday*. Composes *The Poet's Echo*, six settings of Pushkin*, at Dilidjan (completed 23 August).	*The Poet's Echo*, Op. 76.	316-17
	24 October Triple first performances of United Nations commissioned Anthem, *Voices for Today*, in New York (at UN), Paris and London.		318
	28 October First USSR production of *A Midsummer Night's Dream* at Bolshoi Theatre, Moscow.		
1966	*5 April*	*The Burning Fiery Furnace*, Op. 77, Second Parable for Church Performance*.	337-9
	9 June First performance of *The Burning Fiery Furnace* in Orford Church, which is then taken on EOG tour at home and overseas.	Revises *Sweet was the Song the Virgin Sung* (1931).	
	26 August	*The Golden Vanity*, Op. 78, A Vaudeville for Boys and Piano.	
	Triumphant stage revival of *Gloriana* at Sadler's Wells (produced by Colin Graham).		
	11 December	*Hankin Booby*, for wind and drums (later incorporated into Op. 90).	
	Christmas and *New Year* Britten and Pears in USSR for recitals, where they celebrate Christmas and New Year with their friends.		
1967	*1 March* First performance of *Hankin Booby* at opening of Queen Elizabeth Hall, London, Britten conducting.		
	16 March	*The Building of the House*, Op. 79, overture with or without chorus.	
	19 April	*The Oxen* (Hardy carol for women's voices and piano).	
	2 June Opening of the Maltings Concert Hall by the Queen, when *The Building of the House* received its first performance, Britten conducting*.		340-42
	3 June First performance of *The Golden Vanity* at The Maltings by the Vienna Boys' Choir (the dedicatees).		
	17 August	Second Suite for Cello, Op. 80.	
	September EOG participates in Expo' 67 at Montreal with performances of *Curlew River* and *The Burning Fiery Furnace*. Britten and Pears accompany tour, then travel on to New York for recitals. They leave New York on British Council recital tour, visiting Mexico, Peru, Chile, Argentina, Uruguay and Brazil.		
	November	Revises *The Sycamore Tree* (1930) and *A Wealden Trio* (1929).	

October Car trip to Wales, with Pears.
18 October Death in Venice is performed at Covent Garden. Britten is able to travel to London to attend final rehearsal and first performance.
Brief holiday at Barcombe, Sussex.

1974
23 June First European performance of excerpts from *Paul Bunyan* at The Maltings (in the composer's presence).
July
Summer Holiday at Barcombe* with his nurse, Rita Thomson. Serious discussion begins of reviving *Paul Bunyan.*
October Death in Venice performed at The Metropolitan Opera, New York. Britten visits Schloss Wolfsgarten and works on Suite on English Folk Tunes, 'A time there was . . .'*
November
21 December First performance of Third Cello Suite by Rostropovitch at The Maltings.

Revision of String Quartet in D (from 1931).

Canticle V, Op. 89 (Eliot).

403

398

Suite, Op. 90 (for orchestra).

1975 *January*
March
May Canal trip*.
June 28th Aldeburgh Festival, includes revival of *Death in Venice*, and first public performance (on 7 June) of String Quartet in D (1931).
7 July Britten attends revival of *Death in Venice* at Covent Garden*.
9 July Attends performance of new production of *Peter Grimes* at Covent Garden. This was his last appearance at the Royal Opera House.
August
November Visits Venice for the last time, where he completes the composition of the Third String Quartet*.

Sacred and Profane, Op. 91.
A Birthday Hansel, Op. 92, for voice and harp*.

411
404, 405

360

Phaedra, Op. 93.
String Quartet No. 3, Op. 94.

406-7

1976 *1 February* First performance in Great Britain of *Paul Bunyan*, a BBC radio production.
Summer
4 June First British stage performance of *Paul Bunyan* by the English Music Theatre (successor of the EOG) at The Maltings.
12 June Created a Life Peer*.
16 June First performance of *Phaedra* at The Maltings, with Janet Baker as soloist, and Steuart Bedford conducting*.
July Last holiday, in Bergen, Norway*.
Begins work on setting Sitwell poem, 'Praise We Great Men'*.
August
28/29 September Amadeus Quartet visit Aldeburgh and rehearse Third String Quartet* in the composer's presence.
November Continues work on Sitwell cantata, despite increasing physical weakness.
4 December Dies at The Red House, Aldeburgh.
7 December Buried in the graveyard of Aldeburgh Parish Church*.
19 December First performance of Third String Quartet at The Maltings by the Amadeus Quartet.

Version of *Lachrymae* for string orchestra.

Eight Folk Song Arrangements, for voice and harp.

421

413, 414
427

439

Welcome Ode, Op. 95.

431

432-8

1977 *10 March* Thanksgiving Service at Westminster Abbey**.

440

Richard Adeney: 337-9; Aldeburgh Festival: 223, 226, 284, 287, 309, 319, 321-2, 324-5, 333, 340-41, 352, 354-6, 365, 376-9; Mrs Erich Auerbach: 197, 262, 305-8; Berg Collection, New York Public Library: 141-2; Boosey & Hawkes Ltd., London: 61-2 106, 171, 175, 184, 213, 215, 245-6, 248, 301, 320, 351, 364, 371; Boosey & Hawkes Inc., New York: 134, 149, 152-3, 242, 244, 315; BBC Photographic Library: 369-70, 381, 386; Barbara Britten: 14, 23, 25, 30-32, 38, 40, 44, 63, 67, 69, 78, 80, 105, 111, 137, 212, 214, 247, 255, 266, 270, 295, 310, 342; Britten Estate: 1-13, 15-17, 21-2, 24, 26, 35-6, 39, 42-3, 45-8, 52-3, 59, 66, 68, 70-74, 76, 81-6, 88-9, 91, 93-7, 103-4, 107, 109, 113, 121, 134, 143, 158, 176-9, 181, 185-7, 210-11, 216, 220-22, 224-5, 227-30, 233, 239-40, 249, 256-9, 261, 265, 268, 271, 276-83, 285-6, 290-92, 294, 296-8, 304, 311-12, 314, 316-17, 323-4, 363, 366-7, 373-4, 387, 393-4, 398, 421, 431, 436, 439-40; Robert Britten: 18-20, 37; Aaron Copland: 236-7; Joan Cross: 182; Jeremy Cullum: 326; Decca Record Company Ltd., London: 273, 343-50, 372; *East Anglian Daily Times*: 419, 432-5, 437; English Music Theatre Company (formerly English Opera Group): 183, 217, 263-4, 288-9, 303; Faber and Faber Ltd., London: 327-30, 334, 412, 428; Faber Music Ltd., London: 332, 360; Bertl Gaye: 429, 430; Glynde-bourne Opera, Sussex: 188-204, 218; Gresham's School, Holt: 41; *The Guardian*: 92; Dr Jonathan Harvey (photograph formerly

owned by the late Elise Gordon): 353; Princess Margaret of Hesse and the Rhine: 260, 272, 275, 293, 396-7; University of Hull Art Collection: 267; Jane Jacomb-Hood: 358, 361; Nigel Luckhurst: 355, 388, 390, 395, 402, 409-14, 416, 418, 420, 422, 424-6; Robert Medley: 98-102; Dr Donald Mitchell: 28-9, 174, 243; Jack Mitchell, New York: 375; Mrs John Mundy: 145; *Music Review* (Cambridge, May 1971): 157; National Portrait Gallery, London: 27, 231, 274; Old Buckenham Hall School (formerly South Lodge School, Lowes-toft): 33-4, 36, 56; Daphne Oliver: 49-51, 54-5, 57, 135; Ruth Orkin, New York: 205-9; Oxford University Press: 362; Victor Parker, New York: frontispiece; Sir Peter Pears: 87, 112, 155, 170, 180, 232, 234-5, 241, 318, 335-6; Jack Phipps: 65, 162-9, 368, 382, 384, 389, 391-2; John Piper, CH: 385; Mary Potter: 229; *Radio Times* Hulton Picture Library: 178, 216, 219, 238-40, 250-51, 259; Royal College of Music, London: 58, 60; Royal Opera House, Covent Garden: 269, 357, 359; Beata Sauerlander (née Mayer), New York: 79, 108, 110, 114-20, 122-33, 136, 138-40, 144, 146-8, 150-51, 154, 156, 159-61; Enid Slater: 90; Sotheby Belgravia, London: 172-3; Rosamund Strode: 299, 300, 331, 380, 438; Rita Thomson: 383, 394, 399-401, 403-8, 417, 423; Theodor Uppman: 252-4; Beth Welford (née Britten): 64, 77; Eric Walter White: 75, 302.

We would also like gratefully to acknowledge the following copyright owners: Richard Adeney, London: 337-9; Aldeburgh Festival, Suffolk: 223-4, 342, 377-8; B. W. Allen, Aldeburgh: 309; Mrs Erich Auerbach (for the late Erich Auerbach, London): 197, 261-2, 265, 305-8, 312; Edward Mendelson, William Meredith and Monroe K. Spears, executors of the Estate of W. H. Auden: 113; Maria Austria, Particam Pictures, Amsterdam: 220-22, 245-6, 268; A. De Baenst, Ghent: 335-6; Clive Barda, London: 357; Barker's Studios, Lowes-toft: 38; Bassano and Vandyk Studios, London: 2, 76; Sir Cecil Beaton, London: 172-3; Ferenc Berko, Aspen, Colorado, USA: 315; Henry W. and Albert A. Berg Collection, The New York Public Library, Astor, Lenox and Tilden Foundations: 141-2; Bicknell Photo Service, Portland, Maine, USA: 133; *Birmingham Despatch*: 249; Boosey & Hawkes, London: 105-6, 171, 184, 351, 364; Boosey & Hawkes, Inc., New York: 134; Boughton, Lowestoft: 7, 13, 40; BBC Photographic Library, London: 369-70, 381, 386; Barbara Britten: 25, 30; Britten Estate: 19, 28-30, 48, 52, 56, 59, 66-72, 74, 82-6, 88-9, 91, 93-4, 96, 103-4, 111, 134, 210-11, 230, 234, 297, 304, 314, 316-17, 324, 330, 334, 351, 353, 366, 393-4, 421, 431, 436, 439-40; Dominic Photography, London: 333; John Donat, London: 340; *East Anglian Daily Times*: 419, 432-5, 437; Edgar & Co., Lowestoft: 14, 17; English Music Theatre Company (formerly English Opera Group): 212, 217; Mrs. Bettina Ehrlich (for the late Georg Ehrlich, London): 232-3; Faber Music Ltd., London: 332; John Garner, London: 360; Bertl Gaye, Cambridge: 327, 329; Ian Graham, Campsea Ash, Suffolk: 284; Kenneth Green, London: 180, 235; *The Guardian*: 92; Hänssler, Zürich: 266; Eric Hartmann, New York: 242, 244; Roland Haupt, London: 269-70; Princess Margaret of Hesse and the Rhine: 296; Hughes Studios, London: 61, 77; Peter Hutten (for the late Kurt Hutton, Aldeburgh): 216, 239, 259, 280-3, 299-301, 326; *The Illustrated London News*: 320; Lotte Jacobi, Deering, New Hampshire, USA: 149-153; Jane Jacomb-Hood, London: 356, 358, 361; Ford Jenkins, Lowestoft: 226; Humphrey and Vera Joel, Radlett: 227-8, 285; Henk Jonker, Parti-

cam Pictures, Amsterdam: 288-9; Keystone Press Agency, London: 188-9, 195, 218, 303, 379; London News Agency Photographs: 200; Cartoons by David Low by arrangement with the *London Evening Standard* and the Low Trustees: 267, 274; Nigel Luckhurst, Cambridge: 355, 388, 390, 395, 402, 409-16, 418, 420, 422, 424-6; Maiteny, London: 264; Edward Mandinian, London: 177; Harvard University: 183, 185-7, 203-4, 254, 328; Robert Medley, London: 98-102; Jack Mitchell, New York: 375; *Music Review* (Cambridge, May 1971): 157; E. Nash, New York: 138; NBC, New York: 253; National Portrait Gallery, London: 27, 231; Herb Nott and Co. Ltd., Toronto, Canada: 292; Ruth Orkin, New York: 205-9; Frank Otley, Alexander Corbett Ltd., London: 62; Dr. Walter Otto: 398; A. R. & A. Page, Shoreham-by-Sea, Sussex: 87; Victor Parker, New York: 354, frontispiece; Sir Peter Pears, Aldeburgh: 114, 159, 235, 318; Jack Phipps, London: 65, 162-9, 343-50, 352, 368, 382, 384, 389, 391-2; Photo Reportage Ltd., London: 41; John Piper CH, Henley: 385, endpapers; William Plumb, Maiden-head: 1; Mary Potter, Aldeburgh: 229, 230, 287; Press Association Ltd., London: 248, 311, 371; *Radio Times*, London: 78; *Radio Times* Hulton Picture Library, London: 216, 219, 238-40, 250-51, 259; George Rodger/Life Magazine © Time Inc. 1978: 202; Hans H. Rowe, Bergen: 427; Royal College of Music, London: 58, 60; G. Schirmer, Inc., New York: 176; Brian Seed, John Hillelson Agency, London: 322-3; William Servaes, Orford, Suffolk: 325, 406; Allan Sewell, Norwich: 33; Francis Sitwell © 1962: 302; Enid Slater, London: 79-81, 90, 108, 132, 178-9, 181; Rosamund Strode, Alde-burgh: 331, 376, 380, 438; Clive Strutt, Leiston, Suffolk: 341, 373-4, back jacket; Swaine, London: 45; *The Times*, London: 193-4, 196, 198-9, 201, 213, 215; Rita Thomson, Aldeburgh: 383, 399-401, 403-5, 417, 423; Desmond Tripp, Bristol: 241; José Verdeo, Mexico City: 365; Frederick Vogt, Copenhagen: 260; Beth Welford, Alde-burgh: 408; C. Wilson, Lowestoft: 64; Reg Wilson, London: 319, 321, 359; Roger Wood, London: 175, 252, 256-7; E. I. Yavno, Moscow: 313, 367.

BIBLIOGRAPHY

Published sources:

I *Books*

Blythe, Ronald (ed.), *Aldeburgh Anthology*, London, Snape Maltings Foundation and Faber Music, 1972.

Gishford, Anthony (ed.), *Tribute to Benjamin Britten on his Fiftieth Birthday*, London, Faber and Faber, 1963.

Holst, Imogen, *Britten* (a volume in the Great Composers series), 2nd edition, London, Faber and Faber, 1970.

Ludwig von Hessen und bei Rhein, Prinz, *Ausflug Ost 1956*, Darmstadt, 1956 (privately printed).

Mitchell, Donald and Hans Keller (eds.), *Benjamin Britten: A Commentary on his works from a group of specialists*, London, Rockliff, 1952. (Also: Greenwood Press reprint, U.S.A., 1972.)

White, Eric Walter, *Benjamin Britten: His Life and Operas*, London, Faber and Faber in association with Boosey and Hawkes, 1970.

II *Periodicals, catalogues, etc.*

Aldeburgh Festivals, The Programme Books of the, 1948 et seq.

Benjamin Britten, A Complete Catalogue of his Works [Donald Mitchell, (ed.) and John Andrewes], London, Boosey and Hawkes, 1963.

Benjamin Britten, A Complete Catalogue of his Published Works, London, Boosey and Hawkes and Faber Music, 1973.

Heinsheimer, Hans, 'Born in Exile', *Opera News*, New York, December, 1977, pp. 16-17.

[Pears, Peter], *Armenian Holiday: August 1965*, privately printed, 1965.

[——], *Moscow Christmas: December 1966*, privately printed, 1967.

Tempo (ed. Colin Mason), Britten's 50th Birthday issue, Nos. 66-7, London, Autumn/Winter 1963.

Tempo (ed. David Drew), Britten's Sixtieth Birthday issue, No. 106, London, September 1973.

Tempo (ed. Calum MacDonald), 'Benjamin Britten 1913-1976', No. 120, London, March 1977.

White, Eric Walter, 'Britten in the Theatre', *Tempo*, No. 107, London, December 1973, pp. 2-10.

Unpublished sources:

MSS of unpublished works by Britten in possession of the Britten Estate.

Correspondence of Britten with: Mr and Mrs Antonio Brosa; the late Anthony Gishford; Miss Imogen Holst; the late Mrs Elizabeth Mayer; Miss Sophie Wyss (Mrs Arnold Gyde).

Britten's diaries, 1928-38.

Correspondence of Princess Margaret of Hesse and the Rhine.

Study of Britten and Pears in the USA, 1939-42, by Caroline Lippincott ('Conscripts to an Age').

Other books by Donald Mitchell:

with H. C. Robbins Landon, *The Mozart Companion* (1956).

Gustav Mahler, The Early Years (1958).

The Language of Modern Music (1963).

Alma Mahler, Memories and Letters, revised and edited with an introduction (1968).

Gustav Mahler, The Wunderhorn Years (1975)

INDEX

Italic figures refer to pages in the Chronological Table
Works mentioned solely in the Chronological Table do not appear in the Index